MARY AMELIA PALADIN

The Adirondacks that are the Other Half of Me

ISBN: 0-615-29279-8
ISBN-13: 9780615292793

Library of Congress Control Number 2009904439

To order additional copies, please contact us.
BookSurge
www.booksurge.com
1-866-308-6235
orders@booksurge.com

DEDICATION

For my family…

Whose 'other halves' have always been, ADK as well.

My parents- who taught me that I could do anything if I believed it to be possible.
My husband- who has always understood the freedom needed to do those things.
My daughter- who has been a gift to my life and for whom I will always be grateful.
My pets- whose lives enrich mine every single day.

Cover photo of Brant Lake by: Peter R. Cassidy

Interior photos taken by, or courtesy of: Alfred Paladin, Miff Paladin, Alimara Paladin Cassidy, Peter Cassidy, Marion Wanamaker, Stuart Mead.

Sincere thanks for the kind encouragement and help with details to: Doris Scidmore, Arlene Surprenant, Marion Dahl, Mary Mead Rude, Judy Mead Rhoday.

Table of Contents

Foreword

This book is about my time in the Adirondack Mountains. They are the writings and images that I have had drifting around in my mind for many years.

Maybe drifting is not the right word…That would allude to the idea that my mind was clear- free of all other distractions, allowing those ideas to float freely inside my head. How well we all know that our lives do not allow our minds to be blissfully vacant and daydream- like in these times.

This book is the release to freedom for those thoughts. *Whew!*

Please do not think of this as a book about me. It is a conduit for the memories of a very special place. A place that provides a feeling of home. A place that brings forth an emotion that burrows deep inside and never leaves- even if one must leave it. Anyone who lives in, loves, and visits the Adirondacks, understands what I mean. They all have cherished recollections of their very own.

I hope some of the stories I have included in this book will ring a familiar chord or bring back a memory of your time in the Adirondacks. It is my hope that it will bring a nod, a smile, or maybe even a chuckle to you.

In a region so vast, the adventures, memories and observations are, in the scope of things, very compact. Because of that, we, as lovers of this gorgeous place on earth, are connected through them.

Adirondack Blue

The Adirondack sky above
has one distinctive hue.
A bright and vibrant blend of shades,
it's Adirondack Blue.

The water of the many lakes
reflects the heaven's view.
The crimson leaves in autumn's chill,
the stark white birches too.

The mountain peaks in winter's garb
its sparkling crystal dew.
The ice goes out and birds return,
wildflowers rise to view.

The years pass by so rapidly
yet one thing's always true.
There's nothing quite as beautiful
as Adirondack Blue.

Mary A. Paladin

North to the Adirondacks

WHY...
In case you are curious

Why did I write this book?

I have loved the Adirondacks for as long as I can remember. They are a part of who I am, how I think, and what I do.

There is nothing as beautiful as the cerulean blue sky, reflecting from the surface of the lakes that gild the region.

There is nothing as peaceful and amazing as the cry of the loons in the blackened night as they rejoice in their existence.

There is nothing as rewarding as the sight of nature in its splendor, as it changes with the seasons.

And there is nothing as comforting to me as the memories of, and the thoughts about, my time in one of the most beautiful places on earth.

***

There is nothing special, unique, or extraordinary about me, although my parents treated me as if I was, which made me comfortable in my own skin. That is what enabled me to believe that anything is possible; a belief that my dreams would be met if I worked hard. In an era when that was not the normal way of life, when women were to maintain the orthodox status of their gender, I thought it quite revolutionary of my parents to raise me in such a manner.

Mary Amelia Paladin

Ready for a driving lesson on my uncle's boat

In the 1950s, it was almost unheard of to have first children at forty; that is when my parents had me. I had the oldest parents of everyone my age; I also had the best. My survival was dubious, but my parents were full of faith and determination. They were thrilled with my existence, and their unreserved love for me made me who I am.

"Adirondack Tartan"- My Scottish mom made shirts for
herself and my dad that matched!

Being a painter, I find solace in the colors and sights
that I see; there is beauty to be found everywhere, in everything around us…

Being a writer, I love to communicate and think; some
that know me feel I think too much, perhaps that is true…

It is those things that gave birth to and nurtured my love for the Adirondacks.

***

I was born, and still live half of the year, in central Pennsylvania. It is a beautiful area; it is where I was born, and I love it.

I can see the Susquehanna River flow past my home. If I were to throw a stone hard enough, I could hit the water from my back deck.

I grew up next door to a family of six boys and only two girls; I was very good at football, baseball, and war; sometimes the latter took over the prior. That is how I know I could hit the river; I still have a pretty good arm, even if it does jiggle a bit on release...

The mountain ridge outside my front door is a beautiful gift as it changes with the seasons. When the leaves begin to fall, I can see deer on a path that becomes a silent but heavily trodden route. Twice daily, the beautiful, large eyed travelers mosey through our yard on their way to the river.

The other half of me lives for the Adirondack Mountains. I could phrase this statement differently, I suppose, written in the manner such as: I live in the Adirondack Mountains the other half of the year. But that is not how I think of it. The Adirondacks live in me more than I have physically lived in the Adirondacks. They are a part of me, inside and out.

I have traveled to the place that I call my other home, in the majestic, glacial peaks since I was six weeks of age. I cannot tell you exactly how many years that has been, not because of vanity, but because as this book's writing continues, so does the passage of the years. Let us say it is over half a century, but only a little…

Mary Amelia Paladin

In our early Adirondack years

Once Upon a Time
the makings of our fairy tale

When my parents and I started going to the Adirondack Mountains, the ride from my central Pennsylvania home to our destination of Brant Lake, New York took sixteen hours. Obviously, the first few years I do not remember. But when I became aware of the trip, I loved it. It was an adventure.

As a child, I loved the ride "to the lake". That is what we called our trips north; that is what we still call them. I was always so excited that I could not sleep the few hours between the time we packed the car and the time we left.

These days I am still excited and barely sleep before the trip, but now it is because I am the parent, wife, and pet owner. My child is grown and I more often tote pets instead of kids but I, like many women, am one that takes my every role seriously and assumes them for all time.

Getting There
was half the fun

There were no interstates in the early years of our travels; all roads were two lanes and, unlike today, they went in opposite directions.

Travel was slow if you got behind, as my dad called them, a "jug head." You know the type; they crawl along at a snail's pace in the no passing zone…until you make a move to pull up on their side in an attempt to get a bit of a move onward. That is when they decide to strive for the coveted spot of lead car as if we were in the Indy 500. My dad was not one to take chances so (more times than not) we drove many miles behind many jug heads.

My mom was the navigation coordinator. She was also the packing coordinator, the meal coordinator, the entertainment coordinator and the self-appointed coordinator for anything else needing control. She did not drive so she never shared those responsibilities; she just told my dad where to go, navigationally that is.

We left around two in the morning only a few hours after my parents had finished packing our car, or "the gypsy wagon" as my aunt so fondly called it. I was in my footed pjs and wiggled into the narrow sleeping area, left empty so I could lie down. There were no seat belts then, but not as many crazy drivers either, just jug heads.

My mom told me stories. I didn't fall asleep, even though I pretended I did. That prompted her to turn around in the front seat. I enjoyed the silence as I lay quietly, and looked up into the dark sky; I watched the stars and the moon pass, then return.

We drove for many hours in the blackness. My parents would talk to each other in whispered tones that were barely audible. I felt so very safe. We were all together in a magical world enveloped by the night. Eventually, I drifted off to sleep and awoke when the sunrise glinted off the rear window's metal trim (yes metal- not poly something or another).

I changed out of my footed pjs and put on the shorts and top my mom had ready for me in her tote bag; fashion coordination was in the top five of favorite roles. I remember vividly how difficult it was to peel off those sweaty-footed pjs in the skinny, blanketed, sleeping area of our jam packed, wood paneled, gypsy er, red, station wagon.

By the time the sun came up, we were four hours into our trip. Time for breakfast. There was a tiny restaurant, more like a diner, where we stopped each year. It was on the main street of a little town in the Pocono Mountains of Pennsylvania. I do not recall the name of the diner nor the town itself, but the counter woman's name was Ida and my mom talked to her like an old friend. I could tell it made Ida happy. My mom's biggest joy in the world was social coordinator. She truly loved people.

My dad had two cups of coffee and a "cruller," a doughnut to those of my generation. He remarked they had great coffee and the best thing to go with that, was a great cruller. My mother had crumb cake which she drank with tea, very weak tea. She got numerous cups of tea out of one tea bag. As I got older, I wondered whether it was because she really liked weak tea...or if her Scottish frugality spawned the desire. My thrill at the diner was their milk; I have always loved milk. That milk however, was the best. It came out of a big silver machine; it bubbled up and made noise like a waterfall as it filled the glass. It was the coldest milk I have ever tasted.

After that we were on the road again.

The last stop would be a quick break and a bite to eat before our final(*ly!*) destination for that day, my aunt's house in Albany, New York.

We arrived in the very late afternoon; each and every time, she was looking out the window as we pulled into her driveway. Apparently, she could see the gypsy wagon before we could see her house.

She ran out into the driveway to meet us. Literally... she ran; my aunt lived to be 90 and still mowed her own lawn. Hugs, kisses and chatter filled the air as we were rushed, lovingly, into her house.

Inside, the aroma of dinner cooking flooded my senses with the anticipation of seeing "the family" (as my dad put it). We saw them only once or twice a year, and it was great to see the happiness in my dad's eyes when he was with his siblings.

The table was set for eight; the extra table brought in just for the occasion was set for four more. One by one my father's brothers arrived. The number and volume of voices increased steadily. As the night grew later, so did the noise. The happiness of being together took them back to their early years with stories of my Italian immigrant grandparents, whom I had never known. They teased, chided, and backslapped, all as a joyous result of their reunion, or maybe it was the Manhattans.

We stayed in Albany a few days, then it was time to continue northward. I was more than ready. It was not that I did not enjoy visiting my dad's family; it was because I was usually the only child around. My father's youngest brother was the only sibling that had had a child. My only cousin is ten years my senior. It's great now; we compare geneaology finds and try to break through the brick walls in our lineage. But when I was little, those ten years may as well have been a generation gap the size of the Grand Canyon.

So...when my parents reorganized the gypsy wagon and the three of us hopped in, I was in heaven!

Lake George Village
one stop away

The first thing we did when we got as far north as Lake George Village was to pull over and park on Canada Street so my dad could get a hot pastrami sandwich. In central Pennsylvania, hot pastrami sandwiches were not easily available. My dad grew up in an Italian neighborhood in Albany, then lived in Greenwich Village in his twenties. He had grown to love the sandwiches, but they had since become a rare treat to him.

When I think about the ease of parking on the street, midday in July in Lake George Village, I find it nearly unbelievable. We pulled right into a parking space in front of the pastrami stand and got out of the car at a leisurely pace. My dad did not have to flatten himself up against the door of our station wagon to prevent being bumped off in the prime of his life by a souped up, music thumping, muffler thundering vehicle driven by a pierced, tattooed, abnormally blackened haired sixteen year old.

The sidewalks were bustling with people, but the speed of the "bustle" was not feverish. We stood in line and chatted with other vacationers as everyone waited patiently for the steaming hot, foil wrapped, delicacies to be made.

Afterwards, my parents and I took a walk down to Beach Road to look at the view. I remember feeling anticipation grow within me because we were back once again in the Adirondacks. Everything seemed so blue. The sky's reflection poured its cerulean glaze onto the water and a breeze blew white clouds back and forth. If we timed it right, the Minnie-Ha-Ha came in or went out and we were treated to its signature calliope melody.

We walked back to the car ready to continue with the last leg of our trip toward Brant Lake. My belly tumbled with excitement. It rumbled with hunger as well, but the tumble is what I enjoyed and waited for every trip north.

There was one more stop before we reached Chestertown and turned onto Route 8. That was the foot long hot dog stand where my mom and I got our lunch. They were the most scrumptious hot dogs; to my young eyes, they were the grandest hot dogs imaginable. We would split one and an order of French fries for the best tasting lunch of the season. Looking back, I realize that it was not due to the mixture of mustard, relish, chopped onions and ketchup, but the delicious combination of remembrance, anticipation, happiness and excitement that made that hot dog taste so good.

Coincidentally...
maybe destiny

Both of my parents vacationed in the Adirondacks as children. They did not know each other and they came from different areas of New York State. As children, my mother lived on Long Island and my father was from Albany. The odd thing is, both were in the Adirondacks at the same time, in the same years, of the 1930's.

My mother and her family went to Lake Pleasant; my father and his family went to Lake George. My mom was an only child. There were only three of them traveling. My dad was next to the youngest of six children; it must have been a tight squeeze.

My husband has told me stories of he and his brothers in their car. Apparently, "he touched me!" and, "I did not!", was a constant cry. Somehow it is hard to imagine my dad and his siblings like that, but even the best of well-behaved children grow tired of each other at a certain point. I don't mean to imply that my husband was not a well behaved child, but he did cut all the fingers off his youngest brother's Trolls on more than one occasion.

Anyway, when I think of my parents at different, nearby lakes, with different family dynamics, it strikes me with one of those "que sera, sera" feelings. They were both avid horseback riders; the Adirondacks were (and still are) known for its gorgeous riding trails. I have wondered if they were ever at the same stables at the same time twenty years before they knew each other…

***

My husband and I both vacationed in the Adirondacks as children. We vacationed at the same place called Mead's Cottages on Brant Lake and we did know each other. Our paths crossed occasionally but we were quite different so the meetings were short and not necessarily so sweet.

My husband was the type of child who liked to fish, look at swamps, algae, and other gross things that were conducive to the breeding grounds of reptiles and amphibians. To my way of thinking it was a complete waste of precious summer time. It was better to be where the action was: waterskiing, swimming, motor boating and anything else that involved me and all my friends.

I never really gave my husband a second thought back then. Well…that is not true. I did think of him but I thought he was rather odd. He was always looking at and doing the weird stuff he found interesting. I decided very early that he was quite peculiar.

There is a picture (taken of my husband) that hangs on a wall in our home; he was about six. It was taken on the beach at Brant Lake at nighttime during one of the weekly events held back then. He proudly displays a pickerel he caught; his freckled face smiles at the camera with his bright red hair sticking out from under his little baseball cap. In the background is a large group of children playing, running, and laughing; I am one of them. There was no way on earth either one of us would have thought that, so many years later, that photograph would hang on the wall of the home we would make together.

It freezes us forever in a time that was magical. Magical to both of us for different reasons and yet, one in the same. The one in the same is what brought us together as it has done for thousands of other people who come to the Adirondacks.

Twenty years later I decided he wasn't so peculiar after all...

One Particular Year
or, the case of the creeped-out coordinator

The year was 1966. For some reason we reached the diner in the Poconos before sunrise. It was still quite dark and, on that night, quite foggy. I remember the year because my mother had a broken leg. It was a very bad injury. Her leg was in a full, plaster cast; metal rods protruded from both sides of her ankle and knee. It was very heavy and no doubt very hot in the second week of July.

My mother had broken her leg on New Year's Eve…six months earlier. She had decided to be the outside Christmas light replacement coordinator, but that is another story.

My dad had to park our station wagon a block away from the diner because the street was under repair. The only available place was in front of a small, very old, cemetery. My mom seemed a bit uneasy but my father and I assumed her leg bothered her. We promised to bring our things back to the car and eat them there with her. We saw Ida and talked for only a very short time. She asked us to tell my mother that she wished her well. We got the coffee, tea, milk, crullers and coffeecake boxed up and headed back through the fog to our car..

As we got closer, we noticed that the front passenger door was open and the windows appeared to be steamy. One of my mother's crutches was on the sidewalk. Her tartan tote bag was next to the curb, its contents spilled everywhere. When we reached the car, my mom's face was flushed and beaded with perspiration. Her aqua colored culottes were torn at the leg seam. Her casted leg was wedged between the steering column shifter and the snap-down trash receptacle. She looked at us as though it were normal that she was in such a state.

When we asked her what had happened and if she was all right, she reported, in her timekeeper coordinator tone, that she had grown tired of waiting for us. She had decided to come to the diner.

Once we got back on the road and continued northward, we discussed why that predicament had happened. Had she been afraid to wait near that old cemetery?

My mom denied any fear whatsoever.

My dad and I realized we had made a remarkable discovery, the coordinator of the world beyond…she was not.

Parenthood of the Traveling Trunks
…have trunks will travel

My mother was an exceptionally good swimmer. In her teens and twenties she was a lifeguard at various beaches on Long Island. She taught me to swim when I was two.

My dad did not swim; he didn't like the water. I saw him in (what he and my mom called) swim trunks only once. They were an odd pattern of brown, black and white. Not paisley. Not plaid. Tropical maybe. I remember them vividly because it was the only pair he ever owned.

Each year my mother dug them out and tried to talk him into the water but to no avail. That pair of trunks made many trips to and from the Adirondacks but they never got wet. In later years he became an avid boater and loved to cruise Brant Lake on his pontoon; but he did so in summer weight chinos and short sleeved shirts.

As I cleaned out my dad's dresser after his passing, I had to smile. At the very bottom of his bottom drawer, neatly folded, were those trunks. They were still as bright as they were forty years earlier. They had never floated in the cool blue waters of an Adirondack lake, they had never felt the warmth of the Adirondack sunshine. That's just the way my dad wanted it. And that's why they stayed in the very bottom of his Adirondack-bound suitcase.

Tar Paper Makes a Very Nice Home
if you crawl on your belly like a reptile

Everyone has fears. Whether it is fear of the dark, fear of flying, water, animals, and even the fear of stepping outside the safety of their home, everyone has something that makes the hair on the back of their neck bristle, or their belly rise up to meet their tonsils.

It took me many, many years to realize why I am so darned scared of snakes. When I finally figured it out I thought my fear would subside somewhat, but it did not.

One day when I was five, my family went with my uncle over to Schroon River, near Starbuckville Dam, to look at a house he was having built. Being an only child was great most of the time, but there were the occasions when I would have much rather been playing with friends. Looking at the skeleton of a structure interested me, well… not at all.

The ride from our camp was not a long one and it was uneventful. I wish I could say the entire day went that way.

We pulled onto the construction site. It was late morning and the sun was hot and almost mid-sky. My parents ooh'ed and ah'ed.

"How lovely it looks," they said.

"So much progress has been made in the two weeks since we were here last time." "Oh, the roof is almost completed, a good thing because rain is forecast for the next few days."

On and on they went, then exited the car. They inquired, of course, if I would like to join them.

I told them I'd wait in the car.

Actually, I'd rather stick a pin in my eye, thank you.

Off they went, their heads swiveled back and forth. They reminded me of the bobble head dogs that were popular then and found on thousands of rear window ledges. They looked at beams and floors and windows and the kind of stuff adults find ridiculously interesting.

I had taken a coloring book and crayons with me and was perfectly content sitting in my uncle's car. The crayons were new- state of the art. They twisted up and out of a plastic casing, like today's mechanical pencils. There was no need to sharpen them and they did not shed flakes of wax. A budding artist's dream comes true.

Occasionally I glanced in their direction as they studied and commented. My father would give my uncle, his oldest brother, his opinion. They would go back and forth with ideas not requested, or heeded, by either party. Such were the dynamics typical of my dad's large Italian family.

After an hour or so it became quite hot in the car, even with the windows rolled down. I became uncomfortable. I swiveled my crayons down into their casings so that their tips were not ruined from the heat. I began my exit from the vehicle to join my family.

The car had a very heavy door; I needed to put my weight into it in order to make it swing open. My legs peeled uncomfortably off the vinyl seats and I stretched my feet down to the ground. The air outside was not much cooler, but I felt as though I had more of it to breathe than I had had inside the car. The tarpaper underneath my feet had been left everywhere; it seemed as though it went for miles. In reality, of course, it only went a couple of yards until dry, sandy dirt was visible. That was where the bones of my uncle's house began to form its architectural body.

I saw my family down closer to the river's edge; my uncle's arm swept back and forth along the horizon as he showed my parents what he had in mind for the waterfront.

With my eyes in their direction, I took a few steps on the sun-warmed, supple, tarpaper. Then, I felt something different under my feet. It was unlike the flat, flexible surface that it had been one step earlier.

I quickly looked down to assure my footing, and to my horror, there were snakes everywhere! My brain went berserk. I could not see. I could not scream. I could not cry. I could not breathe.

My mind's eye had snakes chasing me as I ran the few feet back to the car. I could not get the heavy door open. I was sure the millions of snakes I had disturbed had their fangs and thrashing forked tongues set on me. Slithering as fast as they could to wrap themselves around my entire body!

I pulled and pulled, my body wracked with fear. A scream finally escaped me, I heard my mother's voice just as the door broke free. I jumped into my uncle's car but I could not get the door closed behind me. I didn't look down. I didn't want to see the mob of serpents that wanted to feast on me. I cried, I shook, I closed my eyes and I waited. I waited for my torturous execution from the army of demons that were slithering up the side of the car to devour me...

The next thing I knew my mother had me in her arms. My father was pulling the tarpaper away from the car and my uncle was stomping his feet on the ground to chase the snakes away.

My eyes still closed, my family repeated that everything was all right. The snakes were gone; there was nothing to worry about.

Slowly I opened my eyes and cast them downward. My family was right. The snakes were gone. The tarpaper, yards and yards away, was tossed chaotically. All I could see were the three faces of my family; concern shrouded them as they all reached out to comfort me.

I stopped crying and took a deep breath. My voice, which had never deserted me before that moment, returned, and I asked to go home.

We did not talk about it much when I was little, just enough to assure me that everything was okay and snakes will not hurt me if I leave them alone. They reminded me of the (universal blah-blah-blah) explanation that snakes are much more afraid of me than I am of them.

Years later, my parents told me that, in fact, there were quite a few snakes; two dozen or more, and with them, their mother. They were small, baby snakes that she had kept under the tarpaper because it absorbed the heat. They were under there because they are cold blooded. I was reminded that snakes are much more afraid of us, than we should be of them...blah,blah,blah.

And so, there weren't a million snakes and they were small snakes at that. Cold blooded? Yes all right, and hooray for their mom who wanted to keep her babies warm; but more afraid of me, than I of them? I tend to think...probably not!

The Adirondacks that are the Other Half of Me

The Snakemobile…

Red Newts, and Fungus, and Slugs
OH MY!

The Adirondack woods are a place of wonder for a child; I was in them as much as possible.

They were cool, shady, and what seemed to be on the surface, quiet. I was sure though, that if I listened very carefully, I could hear noises coming from that motionless soil. There was a hotbed of activity hustling and bustling. Everywhere, one just had to listen very carefully to hear it.

I spent hours in the woods; even when I was still too little to go to the beach alone, I was allowed to venture into the dark recesses of the forest. Not too deeply, but there was no need. There was a goldmine of loot barely a few steps into the wooded wonderland.

Rocks made challenging landing pads; I jumped from bump to bump. Sometimes I didn't land very well and I slipped on the moss that covered many of them.

Pine needles made the flooring. They were soft and forgiving, unless I disturbed them and carelessly rearranged the tiny daggers, which then embedded into, and angered, my skin.

Birch trees were sanctuaries for secret scrolls. Their curling bark boasted invisible transcripts that only those who knew the code could read. I was not allowed to peel the bark; my mother thought it too beautiful, and the trees too sensitive. I still flinch when I see someone peel, even a little bit, the beautiful paper pelt.

Mary Amelia Paladin

The many types of pine trees were the undisclosed combination that made the permanent canopy. The maples, provided the rustle and shade in the spots where old pines had sadly fallen.

The earth was cool and quiet. The giant beech trees were weathered and lumpy, their bark rutted and striped vertically, as if little lightning bolts had decorated the wood-like skin.

Silence was in charge. There was very little sound except for my footsteps and perhaps a small groan as I hoisted a downed log over onto its other side, anxious to see what fabulous population had established itself underneath.

My excitement as to what would be there was strong. I took a generous breath to enjoy the smell of the damp, wet earth.

It was the smell of decay. But it was not offensive; it was exhilarating. It meant life in some form was given by the death of others. The soft, rotted log provided shelter for red newts, fungi and slugs, as well as ants, millipedes, tiny plants of a vast assortment and an occasional boring bee.

My favorites of course, were the red newts. A glorious shade of reddish orange, they seemed to glow against the wet, umber, forest floor. They had tiny spots on their backs and they were very fast. Their little feet had round tipped toes and I was sure that is how they scurried so quickly.

I made many discoveries in the woods of the Adirondacks looking under logs. I learned about moisture and the lack of light; I learned about the life cycle and its need to occur. I learned to respect nature in all of its forms so that we can enjoy the gift it shares with us.

The Adirondacks that are the Other Half of Me

My aim is not to lead you to believe that I came to all these realizations when I was still small and playing in the woods. I'm not scientifically gifted; I'm barely scientifically competent. It took some time for all that logic to settle into my mind and take shape. It did, however, give me the foundation on which I built my respect for, and admiration of, nature in all its magnificence.

The North Pole Goosie
...perhaps it was a gander

I learned the nursery rhyme "Goosie, Goosie, Gander" at an early age. My mom spent endless hours teaching me all the nursery rhymes, but until I started thinking about a title for this little story, I had not thought of it in many years.

In that rhyme, the self-appointed sentry of divine repute- a goose, while on patrol throughout the house of "his lady", tosses an old man down the stairs for not having said his prayers.

The year we visited Santa's Workshop, the home of the jolly old elf himself, I met a goose that was apparently a descendent of that hooligan. His appointment may not have been of the divine sort, but he certainly found it within himself to give me a run for my five-year long life.

What a magical place Santa's Workshop was, secretly nestled in the forest way up the mountainside of White-face. The little village was alive with the sights and sounds any child would expect to see in the place that Santa called home.

Gaily decorated cottages brimming with treats, toys and souvenirs, were tucked amidst the brightly lit trees. Elves scurried about carrying tools and other necessary trappings that any self-respecting Santa's helper would have in tow. The railings of fences were wrapped in green garlands and sleigh bells sounded everywhere.

Mary Amelia Paladin

I remember thinking that it must certainly be the most magical place on earth to live. Where else could one be so close to Christmas all year long? It was August and Christmas was everywhere! Who in the world would have guessed that Santa's *real* Workshop was in the Adirondack Mountains?

In the center of this delightful community of Christmas bliss was the North Pole. The actual Pole itself; it was taller than I was, and it was frozen solid. Not make-believe solid, like plaster or wood painted shiny to look like ice, but really- water turned to ice- frozen solid! It made complete sense to me. Only Santa's home could have a giant frozen ice pole right smack in the center of town in the middle of August. I was so happy we were there to see it with our own eyes, and even better yet, I was able to touch it with my warm, middle of the summer, suntanned hands!

After my dad recorded the event with a million still pictures and as many feet of 8mm movies, it was time to eat. We decided on hot dogs and hot chocolate. Sixty-five degrees or not, there was no doubt- we were in Santa's neighborhood so the beverage of choice had to be hot chocolate.

When the sun began to move lower into the sky we knew it was almost time for us to go back to Brant Lake.

Before we left, however, we took a walk over to the area where the friendly animals strolled freely. Little, crank vending machines were stationed throughout the village. They were filled with pellet shaped animal food. Pop in a nickel, out poured a handful of chow for the docile beasts. My dad held out a handful of nickels and I got busy. For the cost of one nickel my hand overflowed with the tiny tidbits of grassy smelling, food. Nickel after nickel I fed, stroked and cooed to the beautiful creatures.

The animals at Santa's home seemed to have especially good hearing. The second I turned the crank of the little machine, a dozen or more critters came running toward me. I was not the least bit afraid; we always had lots of pets. Dogs, cats, baby chicks, baby ducks, turtles, mice, and rabbits had shared our lives. We loved animals, we still do.

I was on my last nickel when I saw him...

He was an average looking goose. Not especially large or fierce looking; I never would have guessed him to be how (I would soon find out) he was. He was in a hurry and he was hurrying toward me. He waddled as fast as his webbed feet could carry his chesty body; his mouth was open, his tongue was visible, and his eyes were fixed on me.

When I saw his eyes I knew...*that's not a very nice bird.*

He began to honk. He began to flap his wings. He waddled, high speed, directly toward me.

I began to get frightened. I dumped the food. I turned and tried to run.

But, it was too late; he was next to me and he was hungry! Apparently, he had not noticed that I had thrown all the food onto the ground. Either that or he was a meat eater and five year olds were the special of the day.

I side-stepped to save my skin from the honking, spitting, flapping, waddling brute that had set his sights on me. I remember thinking he couldn't hurt me badly, nevertheless I was scared. He managed to get under my feet and trip me, pecking at my hands. I tried to bury them in my pockets but he had grasped my sweater with his huge grey beak. He shook my sweater and me back and forth. The fleshy part of his upper beak undulated like Jell-O falling from a mold. He flung his wings forward and hopped up and down on his leathery legs. He squawked, spit, and carried on terribly. He made one heck of a scene.

My mom, coordinator of bad bird rescues, saved the day by shredding the map we had gotten upon our arrival into tiny pieces. She tossed them off to one side; as the goose ran to snap at the bait, she grabbed me and we high-tailed it out of there.

My dad, the keen photographer, had the choice of coming to the aid of his one and only child or to get it on movie film. I don't want to call much attention to his decision...but we had it converted to DVD three years ago.

Adirondack Kiddie Parks
nobody could see just one!

Years ago when things were not run electronically, when people were needed to role-play, and when children were much different than they are today, there were the "kiddie" amusement parks throughout the Adirondack region. Anyone with children who ever visited the North Country in the 50s and 60s probably visited at least one.

In the years before Great Escape, Adirondack Zoological Park and...well there was not a name change for Frontiertown (probably because the sheriff and his deputies would not allow it!), there were children's attractions called Storytown USA, Animal Land and Frontiertown.

Granted there were others within the Adirondack Park, but these three were my family's favorites so we visited them more often. The North Pole would have been included in this list of toppers if it had not been for that episode of goose gone wild.

***

Frontiertown was a dream come true for kids of the era who were fascinated with "Gunsmoke," amazed at "The Rifleman," had a crush on "Roy Rogers," and were in awe of "Have Gun will Travel".

The park offered cowboys, Indians, rodeo riders, cavalry soldiers, frontier ladies and characters familiar to the West during the era of the Civil War. They also had train and stagecoach rides that could scare the buckwheat right out of unsuspecting parents and small children. On what started as a benign ride toward the little town in the wild frontier countryside, horse-riding, pistol-cracking thieves brought the transport to a terrifying halt. They invaded the peace and tranquility that was, only moments before, enjoyed by everyone on the expedition.

Thankfully, before things went completely awry, the sheriff and his deputies (children, who had been sworn in for the day by the sheriff) came to the rescue. The robbers went to jail, the innocents were rescued, and the deputies lauded. It was a thrilling adventure.

***

Animal Land was my idea of what every child's backyard should be: green grass, shade trees and animals everywhere! I cannot say that I had a favorite animal because I loved them all.

I had saliva, straw, grass, pellets, and dare I say, poop, on my clothes by the end of each visit. I fed animal after animal, petted creature after creature. But I tolerated the alligator wrestling only once. I felt sorry for the poor reptile whose jaws were strapped shut and flipped around like a saddle on a wild horse.

I loved the animals. Big or small I was sure their eyes spoke to me in a language only I understood.

Animal Land in 1955

***

I can say, without any doubt, that Storytown USA was my all time favorite of any of the parks we ever visited in the Adirondack region. Where else could I have met my favorite Mother Goose storybook characters of whom I had grown so fond? My mom read me book after book of nursery rhymes, fairytales and folklore. Imagine my delight when I discovered most of them lived at Storytown USA!

The Old Woman's Shoe was there and, although her children were not visible, I knew they were somewhere nearby. Why else would her shoe need a sliding board in it? Peter, Peter, the Pumpkin Eater had a beautiful pumpkin shell home. The Gingerbread House was truly tempting enough to eat, as long as you did it inside at the snack bar, and did not gnaw on the walls outside.

Moby Dick's mouth was so big I stood on his lip; he was a brightly colored, friendly looking whale. Even Ahab would have liked him.

Mary had her little lamb, but poor Little Bo Peep had lost her sheep. She should have checked the haystack, because Little Boy Blue had an awful lot of sheep at his place. Jack climbed the Beanstalk as the Giant teetered at the top. The Billy Goats Gruff had their own turf and bridge. Humpty Dumpty had his wall and The Three Pigs had joined ranks in the brick abode to avoid the wolf.

It was truly a wonderful place for children of all ages. The colors were brilliant and many. The atmosphere was pleasant and wholesome. The idea that the world was filled with happiness made the best memories for those who enjoyed its magic.

Once upon a time…

***

Two other parks were added to Storytown USA in the lates 1950s and early 1960s: Ghost Town and Jungle Land.

Ghost Town was the rootin', tootin' West, in the 1800s. Complete with a sheriff, who required all boys and girls promise to stay away from guns, to a snake oil salesman who spouted the accolades of products far from useful. It was a bona fide trip back through time.

Bank robberies occurred and shootouts followed. The robbers went to jail, only to be busted out by their no-good friends. Then they all made a fast and furious getaway through the center of town with their guns blazing.

The buildings were authentic, the characters were convincing and the action was plentiful. Dance hall girls shook their can-cans, gunslingers stalked their victims, and residents of the town ambled about in period clothing. Buckboards, stage coaches, wagons and horses traveled past (visiting) families in street clothes.

When we walked down the main street, I felt as though we belonged there. In an odd sort of way, it was almost as if the characters were not "characters" at all. They were neighbors, acquaintances and friends.

Ghost Town was great way to have fun and, learn a few things about history at the same time!

***

Jungle Land was a tropic-like hideaway, removed a bit from the giggles and excitement that danced in the air throughout the rest of the park. It was more serene yet, just as delightful.

Secluded behind a bamboo fence, underneath the veil of lush foilage, were canibals, animals and birds. The path wound through thick vegetation, over a wobbly, rickety suspension bridge, past tree-scaling monkeys, happy crocodiles and elephants that never ran out of water to spray.

The Adirondacks that are the Other Half of Me

My favorite was the hippopotamus; hidden in the vegetation of a small lagoon he bubbled and grumbled. Putting on airs of ferocity, all one had to do was look at his toothy roar to see that a smile was shining through.

***

There were other themed parks for children in the region back then: Land of Make Believe, The Enchanted Forest, Magic Forest, which became a favorite of my daughter's, Gaslight Village, and others beckoned and delighted numerous generations.

The Adirondack kiddie parks were dreams come true for countless children. It was a unique time in history for many reasons and for many people. It was a time when a paper banner, which boasted the name of a themed park and was wired onto the metal bumper of the family car, brought smiles and satisfaction to the happy generations inside.

Pharaoh Lake
a "wild"erness area, the days we rode in

Pharaoh Lake: gorgeous, tranquil, and pristine is but a mere three miles or so from our camp. Well, the trail that is. The gorgeous, tranquil, and pristine part doesn't start to appear until four plus miles later. I promise you, though, you will marvel at its beauty. That is of course, if you are able to live through the blood loss. The bugs are ferocious.

If this were one of my children's books I would tell you that those teeny, tiny bugs have big appetites. They carry teeny, tiny coolers with teeny, tiny Red Crosses on them. They deliver them to a not so teeny, tiny storage vat in which they all lounge on teeny, tiny floats. They wear teeny, tiny bibs; speak a teeny, tiny language to each other; and when they get thirsty, they lean over and take a sip with great, big straws!

***

I cannot pin down the first time I went into Pharaoh, but I was quite small and I rode there. Although the trail into Pharaoh is predominantly a hiking trail, years ago many forms of transport were used if that mode of movement could manage the terrain.

The owner of the cottage community in which we stayed had an old milk truck that children could ride in once they reached a certain size. Every so often he took a group of children for a ride into Pharaoh Lake. It had dents and rusted bumpers. It made such a noise that it was nearly impossible to hear each other. Prior to the old milk truck, he used a Model T truck, but that was before I was big enough to take part and I only remember seeing it, not riding in it.

It was not something that would be easily allowed in this day, for many reasons. Sometimes, when I think of it as an adult and a mother, an icy slice of dread goes up my spine. Then, I recall the thrill and happiness of the experience. I remember the shiver of excitement that scaled my backbone as a child as I reveled in the noise, laughter, confusion and friendship. There was never one minor mishap. And the ride was the greatest fun for all of us. Sometimes things just are; it is because they were meant to be.

Nevertheless, the opportunity for tranquility and contemplation on an Adirondack trail was pretty much shot the days *we* rode into Pharaoh.

The Adirondacks that are the Other Half of Me

Prepping for the ride into Pharoah

Independence Day
Brant Lake style

When I was young, there was a wonderful carnival that occurred in the town of Horicon over the Fourth of July holiday. There were many offerings: food, music, fun for the entire family and, of course, fireworks!

My parents packed a picnic supper for the three of us and whatever friend I had asked to join us. We went into town and enjoyed all the festivities. After supper we got ice cream at one of the booths, then we walked back to our spot on the bank of Mill Pond. My mom, the coordinator of pre-pyrotechnics patience, broke out boxes of sparklers; we swirled and hopped and ran a bit until it was time for the long awaited highlight of the evening. Horicon is not a big town by any means. But when it was filled with so many families, all there to enjoy the festivities, it seemed like a bustling hub of thousands.

***

In later years, I went into the event with my friends. One of our parents drove us the ten miles into Horicon, and dropped us off, not exactly like hot potatoes, even if it did feel that way. They returned later to pick us up. We ate, we drank, we ran, we watched, we followed, and we seldom sat down for a minute. We paused to watch the fireworks but we were still under the momentum of freedom. We made friends there, and we made plans there; some of them came to fruition, some did not. Nevertheless, it did not matter because every experience was important to us as we lived in that particular moment.

Eventually the parent driver returned and we piled into the station wagon, the mini van of the day, minus safety features. We rode back to the northern end of the lake; our voices were loud and excited. We could not wait to get back to camp and share our evening's adventures with those too young to be able to experience their own 'independence' day...

Visiting "General" Stores
generally meant a treat was in store!

I couldn't share my memories accurately if I did not include those about going into to town to the stores. "Town" either meant Chestertown or Horicon, although we usually referred to Horicon (Brant Lake) as "the village".

As a youngster I did not go into either one much unless my dad was at the lake or if I rode in with one of my friends. My mom did not drive, and with the store on site where we stayed, there was no real need to go to town. However, it was a treat when I did go. I had favorite stores that were typical of the time and the region.

***

Fish's in downtown Chestertown was one of them. Even as a very little girl the floors creaked as I walked on them. I found it fascinating and I remember thinking that it would not be a good place to play hide and seek; there were way too many noisy give-aways.

Immediately upon entering, I ventured over to the candy aisle to pick out a few things for the ride back home. Routinely, I chose pretzel sticks, black licorice whips, and caramel bull's eyes. The cost was ten cents. Each visit my parents encouraged me to pick a little book, or comic, as well.

My mom talked to Mr. and Mrs. Fish while I took my (good ol') time in selecting my reading material. I liked to read books more than comics; the bubbles with the dialog seemed too helter, skelter to me. I did like all the pictures though. The colors were bright and the visual action that took place interested me very much. But more often than not, I picked a little book. It had to be a book that had beautiful pictures and a story line that did not distract from the illustrations. It had to be a book that had room on its pages for one little girl.

***

Brant Lake General Store (Steinman's, Daby's, Burnett's, Cronin's, Kenovan's, Smith's, Barton's- however you think of it) was a favorite spot of, not only mine, but many other people as well. It was Burnett's when I was a child and it did not change drastically over the next forty or so years. Of course, there were the updates of business machines, needs for different types of merchandise, some self-serve allowances and even an attached liquor store. Fortunately though, it did not get lost in the progressive evolution that so often steals away the very thing that draws us nearer.

The old, worn, wooden floors squeaked underneath my feet. When I was very small, and health department regulations were yet to be imposed, we were allowed to enter barefooted. The big, old, screened door creaked on its springed return and slammed behind us as we walked down the main aisle.

Again...I detoured toward the candy section to select my treats. At the General Store I almost always picked a (full sized, five cent) Sugar Daddy and five cents worth of candy. The loose pieces were put into one of those teeny little brown bags, which for some reason I loved, almost as much as its contents. They were like little treasure bags brimming with special things to be savored.

There were offerings of ice cream bars, Fudgesicles, Nutty Buddy's (my mom's favorite) and sherbet Rocket Bars, among others. But I was content with my little brown stash bag filled with Atomic Fireballs, B.B. Bats, Nickl Nips or whatever my sweet tooth ached for on that particular day.

In later years, my daughter's childhood years, it was Daby's. It held the enchantment of the many years gone by although it kept up with the needs of changing times. Thankfully, doing that did not eliminate the novelty of its ambiance of the general store feel we had all known and loved for so long. Its door still creaked as the spring stretched then recoiled. Its dull, worn floorboards still creaked as they had through decades of many pairs of feet, bare and shoed. Its shelves echoed the hushed whispers of children who lined up in front of them, selecting treasures to be dropped into small brown bags. Its silent walls protected conversations shared over generations, amongst friends, neighbors and families.

Although ownership changed one more time, the Brant Lake General Store remained a genuine representation of "the general store" found throughout the Adirondacks. A crucial element in many lives, chronicles, and memories.

In 2006, it was destroyed by fire.

When fire ravages and ultimately takes the life of a building around which the vitality of a community has evolved for over a century, there is no way to replace it. Although known as a building for commerce, for trade, for business- whatever it may be have been called- it was not merely a building. It was a friend; a friend that perished never to return. Its construction, not merely walls and windows, but a fragile body, with eyes to the soul of a community.

Brant Lake General Store had been an icon since 1865 (rebuilt in 1894). And even if one day another store were to rise from the ashes, the one that was consumed by the angry tongues of orange, can never be replaced…

Ah, Sunset…
Mountain Lodge that is

Years ago, the New York State legal drinking age was eighteen. I could not wait to be eighteen and "officially" go to a bar. While underage, I did not sneak into Sunset or any of the other alcohol serving establishments of the area. I did not really have the desire to go to one; in my home state of Pennsylvania, the legal age to consume alcohol was twenty-one. Being allowed to drink at eighteen seemed like pretty good deal to me. I did visit Sunset for that reason when I became of age, but it was mostly because of the fun I had there and it included very little alcohol.

It was a great place to go with friends, to meet and make more friends. We met young people from all over the world who were on Brant Lake, as counselors at the various summer camps: Read, Brant Lake, and Point O' Pines. We made friends with young people that lived in the area year-round and we made friends with young people whose families vacationed on Brant Lake. It was always fun. Each year we met new people and were reunited with those that returned annually.

***

Driving to Sunset by boat was everyone's favorite thing to do. It was the novelty of being able to hop out of the boat at an actual destination, much more interesting, challenging, and rewarding than one's own dock! That may sound silly, perhaps, but it's true. My group of friends did it, my family did it, many people did it; as I reminisce with others that remember it, everyone else loved it as much as I did. We would boat over for pizza. We would boat over for a beer (I didn't drink beer- but kahlua and club generally hit the spot). We would boat over just for the heck of it. They were great times, fun times, carefree times.

***

Going to Sunset on the water was not always done by motorboat...

One evening during a game of cards, a few of my mother's friends accepted a wager. The challenge was that they had go to Sunset, a few miles down the lake, and they had to do so via the water. They also had to have a piece of paper signed by the bartender to attest to their arrival. They then had to return, via the water, with that proof.

They set off from our end of the lake. They wore their sunhats for protection. The hats, in addition to the old, black, inner tubes were the daywear fashion signature of my mother's group of friends. No doubt liquid refreshments had been stowed in the cooler for the ride. The wind, which blows from the southern end toward the northern end, made it a difficult trip for them.

Not only was the wind a deterrent, but also the mode of transportation produced a bit of a handicap. The trio took a two-person paddleboat; one of the travelers rode on a kiddie float that was tied to the back. They paddled, they rested, they paddled, and they rested, eventually reaching Sunset by afternoon.

They got the required evidence of their arduous journey. A beverage that sported a generous drape of condensation and emitted a lovely aroma of hops, accompanied the well-deserved break.

Pleased with themselves, they set off and headed north, much easier with the wind at their back.

Paddle, paddle, paddle. All went well for a very short time, until the skies opened up and the rain came down.

Fortunately, one of their sons came to the rescue of the weary wanderers. They got in his motor boat; the two-seater and the float bobbed in its wake as they made their way to the northern end of the lake.

Although they were drenched, their spirits were certainly not dampened. 'Twas proof they had sought, 'twas proof they had gotten.

Mary Amelia Paladin

"Tons of Fun"
My mom & friends: a typical Brant Lake bay, floating day!

Serial Killer at Large
Terrifying

In July of 1973, a teenager from Schenectady, NY was killed while on a camping trip with three friends in the area of Speculator, which is not that far from our camp. Within a day of the terrible tragedy, the entire North Country was on edge. It was a brutal and intentional murder. Serial killer Robert Garrow was the assailant and he was on the loose.

In those days we did not have TVs in the cabins. But still, word spread quite rapidly throughout the region.

My mother and I were alone that week; my father had gone home. Our cabin didn't have real locks on the windows and had only a hook-type lock on the screened door. We had never had an occasion to be concerned before but, needless to say, we were a bit nervous. The knowledge of this tragedy a mere half an hour from our lakeside refuge was frightening. The North Country is big country. But we decided it was not big enough when we heard that a roadblock had been set up near the spring in town.

The dread grew more intense when a friend of ours was stopped in her orange VW and questioned. Garrow drove an orange VW hatchback. We knew that police dogs, and helicopters had gotten involved in the pursuit and we knew the areas of the search had grown and gotten closer.

We emptied the cupboards of all the pots and pans and any other item that would make noise; we strung them across the windows and doors. Obviously, this method could not stop an intruder but we thought it may deter any attempt. The two cabins on either side of us followed suit and we all felt a bit safer.

It was known that Garrow had visited his sister in Mineville. A few days later, it was there, he was captured.

After eleven worrisome days, the fear that had spread across the lower Adirondacks, and one of the largest manhunts in New York state history, ended. With much relief and gratitude, my mother and I, as well as campers throughout the Adirondack Park, sighed a breath of relief and caught up on lost sleep.

Elvis
has left…

August 16, 1977 was a picture perfect day in the North Country…. I had just gotten out of the lake and was squeezing the gallon of water out my long, dark hair. (I say that wistfully since now it is short, and ah…not naturally dark.) I was waiting for the water to stop running down my back so that I could, once again, fold myself onto my beach towel and resume my obsession with achieving the perfect suntan. I turned my back toward the direct sun and waited patiently as the last few rivers ran from my hair.

Suddenly, a child's scream ripped across the crowded beach.

I whipped around in an attempt to discover from which direction the scream had originated. Everyone turned toward their children. They needed to confirm their safety. What happened? Who was that? Why was it?

Halfway across the beach I spotted one of the young girls on the ground. She had collapsed in the sand.

She was crying profusely and shaking her head back and forth. She repeated, "no,no,no. It just can't be true." A copy of the New York Daily News was scattered on the sand next to her.

Her mother reached her side and propped her into her own folded legs. She stroked her daughter's hair and spoke softly to her. The young girl sobbed and the mother comforted.

They were completely alone yet they were not.

This young girl, quite a few years my junior, many years Elvis Presley's junior, was heartbroken. Her idol was gone. The loving mother comforted her child as she mourned an enigma whom she did not know, yet admired, and in her own way loved.

Sadly, I realized that somewhere else far away from the peaceful blue lakeside, another mother was comforting another little girl. A little girl who would miss that same enigma whom she did know very well, and loved as only a daughter can love a dad...

Ticonderoga
historical and hysterical

Ticonderoga...the name does not go unnoticed when mentioned. Anyone interested in American history can tell you that Ticonderoga and the area surrounding it is steeped in amazing historical events. Three nations battled on it and many people died there. Much was gained and much was lost there.

It was named by Native Americans, the name means land between two waters; those waters are Lake George and Lake Champlain. Ticonderoga is located where northern Lake George runs into Lake Champlain via the La Chute River. The importance of its location (the control of the North/South waterway) resulted in the construction of Fort Ticonderoga by the French about 1755. A fascinating saga of events took place in, or around, Ticonderoga. You can feel the spirits, and hear the whispers, of those thousands from all nations who fought there. It is awe-inspiring. I could go on for pages about it, but there have been many wonderful books written on the subject. I could not begin to do justice to the explanation of what the region's role played in our country's history.

***

Ticonderoga also has a breathtaking golf course. I mean that literally as well as figuratively. It is very hilly, perhaps mountainous is more apt, but it is gorgeous. It is near the site of the Snowshoe Battle fought by Roger's Rangers in 1758.

My dad loved to golf. I am not sure if he was a good golfer or not, but regardless of that, he loved it. I went with him a few times but I soon discovered I do not like to golf. There are so many beaches on which to lounge, and so much water in which to swim in the Adirondacks- why would I want to walk around a blistering hot patch of grass that is the breeding grounds for gnats, snakes, and frustration? While staying on Brant Lake my dad golfed frequently. He was not a beach enthusiast so off to the course he went.

The golf course at Ticonderoga Country Club is not for the faint of heart; fortunately, my father was a very healthy man during his golfing years. He was a trim, energetic man without even one ounce of body fat on his bones. Unfortunately those particular genes did not tumble into my pool. My dad was not a golfer who rode in a cart. He walked the courses. He loved the heat, he loved the sunshine. He loved to chew peppermint gum while he golfed and he enjoyed the nineteenth hole very much when he was finished.

One year my mom bought him a self-propelled mechanical golf "caddy" for his birthday. Back then it was "high tech" and "futuristic". It was beautiful: a shiny silver contraption into which his entire golf bag strapped tightly. My dad was still able to walk the course the way he enjoyed, but the "caddy" carried his clubs. It had a control panel of sorts that allowed the golfer to adjust the speed of the machine to the desired pace. My dad always walked rapidly so the caddy was moving along at a swift rate right next to my father as he moved from shot to shot. The caddy was parked while the club was selected and a shot was made. A light twist of the knob and golfer plus caddy were on their way to the next site.

My father had a friend at the lake: a fellow Pennsylvanian, neither of them were Pennsylvanian by birth. I am sure it was divine intervention that they both ended up at Brant Lake, that they loved to golf, and that they became such good friends. It was with that friend that one of the funniest occurrences in my dad's life happened while golfing at the course in Ticonderoga.

As I mentioned, the course is very hilly. My father and his friend were on one of the holes down in the valley at the time it happened. They didn't tell us which hole it was but they did say that when they looked toward the nineteenth hole, it seemed like it was a million miles away- straight up.

My dad had parked his caddy to the side of the thoroughfare.

Apparently, upon my father's approach to his beautiful, new gadget, he bumped the controls. The machine took off at full throttle and tore across the grass, spewing golf clubs as it went. My father ran full speed behind it attempting to collect his clubs as he ran after his new toy that whizzed across the course. The chase continued until the caddy finally ran into a tree.

For years afterward the story was told and retold. Instead of becoming dull or monotonous, it became funnier each time.

To envision my father chasing his out of control caddy across the mountainous golf course while it spit clubs everywhere still makes me laugh.

Each time I drive past the Ticonderoga Country Club, I think of my dad and his friend that day. A wide smile- my

Mary Amelia Paladin

dad's smile- creases my face and a chuckle brightens my day. Fortunately, those genes did tumble into my pool.

Breathtaking
the beauty of it all truly astounds me

When September arrives, the Adirondack Mountains begin to transform.

June, July and August hold a special place in the hearts of thousands of people who wisely choose the Adirondack Park as their summer vacation destination. However, it is in the ninth month of the year when the value of nature's gift is revealed.

September may begin as if nature's thermostat for August had not been turned down. The heat can be just as warm as a July beach day. But after Labor Day, most people have a difficult time finding the time to grab a chair and saunter to the water's edge. There is school and work that must be attended, there are appointments that must be made and kept, and there are preparations that must begin for the upcoming winter months ahead.

The days begin to pass. Jackets and long pants have taken priority in wardrobe selections. The breeze off the water has acquired a nip. Although the water sparkles like diamonds when the sun dances on it, the desire to bask in its silken coolness does not pull on the heartstrings of your soul.

What does pull on your heartstrings is the gratitude for the beauty of the Adirondacks.

The chill at night spawns the blue sky; its brilliant marriage with the leaves that boast so many colors glorify the sunshine that soothes the chilly pinch during the day. The mountains- some craggy and sharp, some smooth and rounded- show off their autumn dress. The lakes become bluer as they reflect the glorious sky; their edges are a saturation of brilliant ribbons as the foliage drapes its image on the surface. The rushing rivers carry the lively colors of the renegade leaves that fell to earth early. Their cold waters carry them past the stately bearers that have held them close all year. The peak of autumn foliage is on display as the calendar slips into October. Shortly afterward, a dramatic change of season barges in. It means that winter is close behind.

The breezes become winds, the waters turn choppy- then brittle. The vibrant colors fall from the lofty branches that once nourished them. Even though the colors fade, the mystery that is left behind those leaves can be seen.

The naked trees stand bravely. Skeletal in appearance, their bare branches afford a panorama of the mountains, lakes, rivers, and gorges. Their bones are crooked, gnarled and bowing in the icy winds. Their marrow thins, but it will flow again in springtime to the fingertips that will give birth to new life. The pines stand guard over their vulnerable comrades and lend their permanent hue to the landscape.

Whether it is the remarkable colors of fall, the many greens and the cerulean blue of the summer months, or the crystalline white that glistens on peaks and on frozen expanses of water, the Adirondacks truly are…breathtaking.

BTW
…not bacon & tomato on white

For those of you that are of my generation, who may not be caught up with the code of today's young people, BTW stands for "by the way". My daughter and her friends are completely abbreviated in all they do and say. I felt it only appropriate to steal a bit of their thunder and title it as such; it is about them.

My daughter, who is now in her early twenties, loves the Adirondacks; she is adamant in her feelings. I have known it for a long time, since she first arrived on the scene in the North Country at five weeks of age. She became verbal early, and the topic of the lake and the Adirondacks have set precedence over many of her life's decisions.

She told me about a remark a friend of hers made. He told her that he lives in a house elsewhere but his real "home" is at the lake. She thought that was pretty cool because she feels the same way; the rest of her friends do too.

The young people of today keep in contact all year long online, text messaging, and cell phone calls. Nevertheless, friendships must be nurtured and time spent together secures the bonds that last a lifetime. Gone are the days of letter writing and waiting a (terribly long) week to hear from a summer friend. Gone is the emptiness felt as the car pulls away and that friend's face gets smaller while the distance gets bigger. That seldom happens these days…a wonderful thing this technology.

One of those friends came to spend Labor Day weekend at the lake with us. She and her family had not been able to come to camp that year; their camp sat dark all summer.

My daughter's friend climbed the rocky road to our camp, burdened down with a huge duffel bag; as she drew nearer, the smile on her face spoke volumes. We opened the door to welcome her. The first words from her lips were not a greeting, were not a groan of fatigue, were not squeals of delight.

After her deep sigh, the first words spoken were, "It's so good to be home…"

We hugged her, we laughed with her, we fed her, and we talked together as though she were there only yesterday.

That is what makes this place home. It is home to me, it is home to my husband and daughter, and it was home to my parents. I truly believe that the North Country has a way to become home to everyone and if (even) one person never felt a connection to any other place in the whole world they will find a feeling of "home" in the Adirondacks.

To Love a Place

In the Beginning
my uncle shared with us, his heaven on earth

The first time my parents and I went to the Adirondack Mountains we went to Mead's Cottages on Brant Lake. It was in mid September 1955; I was six weeks old.

My uncle had a camp there and he had offered it to my dad for our use. My dad was a bit unsure. It was in the middle of nowhere; my dad liked cities. It was near water, not his favorite thing. There were thousands of bugs; he was deathly allergic to bees. But my mom was in favor of it so we headed north.

From what I was told it was rather chilly that particular week; my mother had me bundled up in a big way. I've seen pictures and it's somewhat difficult to distinguish if I am animal, vegetable or mineral. Considering what many six week old children look like, that is probably not an uncommon query.

We made the rounds: Lake George, Lake Luzerne, Lake Vanare, Lake Pleasant, Gore Mountain, Swede Mountain, Tongue Mountain, Speculator, Prospect, as well as others. My father was an avid photographer. So not only did we make the rounds throughout the Adirondacks, but we also have hundreds of great pictures to remember all the adventures.

Mary Amelia Paladin

As I looked through his mountains of perfectly categorized photographs for this book, I laughed, I cried and I remembered what a lucky kid I was.

There I am, in my mom's arms resting in the crux of a large tree on the shore of Lake George, her face radiant. There I am in my dad's arms in that same tree, his smile (almost) hides the nervousness of being a new dad. There I am at Lake Pleasant in a double pointed woolen knit hat, bundled so deeply that I look like a starched baby bunny with a cheek full of carrots.

There I am in a stroller in front of Toni and Alf's on Lake Vanare. This is a picture that is one of my favorites as it portrays our early days as Adirondack enthusiasts.

There I am in a carriage at the top of Tongue Mountain, the anxiety still pressed on my mother's face. Often throughout my life the "The Tongue Mountain story" was told. My mom was petrified as we climbed our way to the top. My father's car had begun to overheat. Her fear grew as she looked *way* down below. She was convinced that the three of us were to plummet to the base, never to be seen again. She should have been worrying about the rattlesnakes that find Tongue Mountain the summer resort for serpentine subathing.

We had a wonderful time that year I was told, and the pictures, which I will cherish always, tell me it was true.

***

Thus began our lifelong tradition of staying at Mead's Cottages on Brant Lake. As the years continued, we outgrew my uncle's camp and began to rent cottages and eventually bought our own little place at Mead's.

The Adirondacks that are the Other Half of Me

As I write this, more than fifty summers later, I sit only a few feet away from the water, the sand, and the tiny camp where my love affair with Brant Lake began.

Brant Lake
there's no place like home

My husband overlooking Brant Lake from Stevens
Mountain

Mary Amelia Paladin

When I hear the two words Brant Lake, or merely see them in print, so many feelings come to mind that my head spins. Granted, it *is* just the name of a place. I'm not sure how a name can stir such feelings. Nevertheless, since I was very small and able to connect the name Brant Lake with my existence on this earth, I knew that it was a part of me.

Brant Lake is a gorgeous lake. In my opinion it is, of course, one of the most beautiful, peaceful, and inviting places on the planet. It's a small lake in the scheme of things, but that has always been one of its attractions to my family. The water is calm and friendly on most days; even on the days that the whitecaps roll and churn, it's not terribly daunting. It sparkles like diamonds in the morning as the sun rises between Number Eight and Stevens Mountains. Its silky covering smoothes into dark velvet as it disappears behind Prickly Ash and Sand Mountains.

I haven't lived on Brant Lake in the winter but I have visited. Even when it is ice covered and groaning, when the daylight provides but a small bit of warmth, the lake feels like a friend. No, I have not passed a winter next to its wind and wonder but I hope to someday. I know its thick, expansive ice provides beauty worth more than a thousand words.

The Adirondacks that are the Other Half of Me

My daughter's winter visit to our beach on Brant Lake

We Traveled the Diamond-flecked Road
no yellow bricks needed here

Our camp is at the northern end, on the western side of Brant Lake. It's not on State Route 8 but on the less traveled side of the lake: Palisades Road. It's a road that was paved in macadam that had (what may have been) quartz or micah chips.

As a very small child I thought the road was made with diamonds in it. That's what my parents told me, as we turned off Route 8 and began the twisty ride toward the other side of the lake.

"Oh my," they said, "here we are once again; it appears there have been even more diamonds sprinkled on the road."

I was captivated by the magic. How did all these diamonds become so small and find their way into the blacktop of this winding road? Who did this each year?

If we arrived in the daylight, the sunshine reflected off the tiny, jeweled flecks. They threw beams of brilliance that bounced from the metal hood of our car and into our narrowed eyes. If it were nighttime, the headlights made the glistening, mineral trinkets dance everywhere, all the way around the lake. It was as if they sparkled in celebration of our return; another wonderful year had arrived!

***

Mary Amelia Paladin

Many nights my friends and I lay down on that less traveled road and looked in wonder at the vast, open blackness above. It was not dangerous to do so I must report. Just as the diamonds in the road had captivated me in earlier years, the diamonds that I had discovered in the sky were equally breathtaking.

My daughter and her friends have done the same invigorating thing frequently in more recent years. It's a ritual of sorts; it just happens; it's not taught, it's realized.

The sight of those twinkling gems spilling from the deep, black velvet bag in which they are hidden is mystifying.

And maybe, just maybe…falling from the sky, is how the road was embossed with their beauty.

Mead's Cottages
On Beautiful Brant Lake

That is how the wonderful place that introduced us to the Adirondacks was advertised. The slogan, in its entirety, meant so many wonderful things to so many people, that I alone cannot begin to explain it and do it suitable justice.

In all honesty, the reason it was imperative that I put this book together is due to the existence of the bustling little lakeside retreat. The majority of my experiences in, and passions for, the Adirondacks began there.

There were so many unique aspects and things about the place that I only hope I can portray them well enough. If I am successful at that, you will be able to envision the wonderful, magical, place that it was. I cannot profess to know the exact history or beginnings of Mead's Cottages but I can share with you what I do know.

***

Ruth and Norman Mead started the little colony of housekeeping cottages in the late 1940s. They returned to the Adirondacks with their first two children after living in Florida where Norman had run a gas station (featured as an ex-GI businessman in The Saturday Evening Post, April 1946).

It all began with one cottage that was pulled down a frozen Brant Lake. Ruth's great grandfather, Captain Austin Ross had built it. He was a civil war veteran and the first steamboat operator on Brant Lake. The cottage was situated in a spot on the waterfront; later, more followed.

Some cottages were built, some were converted from prior uses, and all were given names: The Martha Ray, formerly an icehouse owned by a couple named Martha and Ray; The Towers, formerly a water tower. The Mary-Lou, named after oldest daughter Mary Louise (originally named Castle High, and the one that was moved down the lake); The Rec Hall, a recreation hall; The Rest Haven, a restaurant; The Beachcomber, a lakeside snack bar, The Green Trim, you guessed it, trimmed in green. The Red Trim, was renamed The Joy See by a zealous guest; I'd bet someone named Joy(ce) was involved; The Duplex was a double cottage; The Lake Shore, The Bay Pines, The Knotty Pine, The Hilltop, The Birches, and The Shangri-La, bore names for which I am sure there was a significance. I could take a guess at them, but they would be half-remembered stories and I would rather not take that liberty.

In the earliest days, the Meads and their (eventually) four children, lived in a cottage or tent in summer while they worked on the project. They rented a house in town for the winter. The summertime community evolved over the years as they labored tirelessly creating a vacation spot that was family friendly, exciting, fun, and wholesome.

"Mead's Cottages on Beautiful Brant Lake" was the advertising slogan used, but the best method was by word of mouth. Vacationers from many northeastern states traveled annually to the lakeside resort to enjoy a taste of Adirondack living. So popular was Mead's, that a waiting list for cottages was kept. Additional campsites were started in the fifties.

The Adirondacks that are the Other Half of Me

Norman, an inventive and outgoing man, knew everything that happened within the cottage neighborhood and prided himself on running a decent operation. He loved children and aspired to remember every name, but it was Ruth who usually reminded him quietly.

Quietly is how Ruth handled her part in the family venture and she did so with expertise and consideration. Norman was the idea man; Ruth was the one who made the ideas happen. They were a great team.

Norman died in 1975; a few years later Ruth closed the very popular general store that was on site. In the late 70's, after discussing it with her children, she decided to sell the cottages to private owners. Lengthy preparations followed but Ruth, not a stranger to patience, worked out all the details. Four cottages, one for each child, were spared. They still bear signs with the original names. Ruth passed away in July 2008; the campsites still exist and the cottages, with small tracts of land, are owned by others.

Nevertheless, if one were to listen carefully (or perhaps be lucky enough to remember it) the soil, sand, and water still echo with the sounds of happiness and friendship that was once Mead's Cottages.

Mary Amelia Paladin

Postcard of Mead's Cottages

Cottage Dwellers
we got much more than a roof over our heads

My family stayed in many of the cottages as well as a few of the all season homes that Norman had built in the area. We also stayed in the small apartment over the garage of their home on occasion if no cottages, camps or houses were available. We extended our vacations often and sometimes such was the case.

We were Adirondack "cling-ons". Still are…

The cottages at Mead's were important settings in my childhood as they were for many kids. They not only sheltered our bodies, they sheltered our childhood as well. We could be on our own, and we'd be safe. We could be ridiculous, yet we'd be sincere. We could be wild, but we followed rules. We were able to be the children we were as the setting and surroundings contributed to the adults we'd become.

***

"The Mary Lou"

It was originally called Castle High many, many years ago; it did not sit on the prominent point on which it has been for the last half (or so) century. Ruth Mead's great grandfather Captain Ross began its construction a few years before that. It had two rooms, no electricity, and no running water. The cottage was located on Beaver Pond Road and was pulled onto the northern tip of a frozen Brant Lake then pulled (just a bit south) on the ice to its final place of rest.

In the early days of the business' development, the Mary Lou (renamed for their oldest daughter, Mary Louise) was moved to its present location and was home to the Mead family. They lived in it, as they did in others at various times, while they worked on unfinished cottages.

We stayed in The Mary Lou a few summers. It's situated on a somewhat rocky point of land on a ledge right next to the lake. It was an adorable cottage; it was painted white with red trim around the windows and doors. It had a screened-in sitting room on the front side, which afforded a beautiful view of Brant Lake and a lovely breeze that blew in softly as it danced over the lake. In front of it, a long dock extended out over the water. It had numerous slips to accommodate boats and there were gas pumps that guests on site, boaters, and others on the lake, could frequent. It was a busy spot with people, children, water skiers and boating enthusiasts everywhere. Back and forth, up and down that small ledge they went, sun up until sun down. There was never any lack of traffic, whether on foot or in watercraft.

It was a great cottage in a great location. It was perfect for an only kid like me who paid attention to, not only my own business, but to that of other kids as well. It was a "happenin'" place to stay, and you can be sure I never missed anything that was happenin'!

"The Duplex"

The Duplex was a large, long, double, cottage. We stayed on the side nearest the path through the woods. I loved to play in the woods, plus, it was a straight away shortcut to my friend's camp on the other side of the trees. We knew that path as well as all the other ones that twisted through the woods at Mead's. We could walk or run it with our eyes closed, in the pitch dark, without a flashlight. We knew every stump, bump, log and rock on those paths.

***

There were two bedrooms in our side of the Duplex; none of the walls between any of the rooms went to the ceiling. I found this very interesting. The supports were exposed, which made the fiberboard walls very easy to climb.

One rainy afternoon, my friend and I got up on top of the wall above my bed and jumped down onto the bed together. After we had worked up a sweat and the bed didn't sound as though it would withstand much more, we decided to continue one at a time. We had a blast, of course, until the bed gave way and crashed to the floor. Panic stricken, we clamored to come up with a plan.

My friend, tiny little thing that she was, crawled under the bed and tried to lift it up a bit while I looked at the damage. When that didn't work, both of us laid on our bellies and propped one side of the bed frame on our heads. It was too dark to see underneath; I told her to hold it up herself until I got a flashlight. She cast me a look of disbelief that was edged with a bit of fear but she got brave and I got a flashlight.

My dad's heavy-duty flashlight blasted its beacon under the bed when I pressed the button. We looked in disbelief. We looked at each other. Then we laughed. We laughed because we knew we could patch it up.

My friend shimmied under the bed. She pushed the debris out from underneath and she shimmied back out. I gathered it up and made a "leg" for the bed. I used my mom's masking tape and strapped it together. I held the corner of the bed up with my head as she shimmied back underneath, "leg" in tow. She lodged it into place with a bit of a grunt and, to save her from yet another shimmy, I pulled her out. We looked at each other and promised we'd tell no one.

I often wondered if anyone had ever taken the tape encased leg apart to read one of the books that had held that bed up.

***

The Duplex was also the cabin in which the 'bat attack' took place.

My (same) friend and I were looking for an adventure. We were not sure what that was to be, so we went to the cottage to get some sweatshirts; we needed to be ready for anything. I went into my bedroom and got two sweatshirts while she went into the bathroom.

Suddenly, a scream pealed throughout the cabin and my friend shouted, "not my hair! Not my hair!"

I ran to the bathroom where she was huddled behind the door with her hands over her head. I saw the terror in her eyes at the same time I felt the tiny puff of air move the ringlets on the top of my head.

She cried hysterically as she covered her beautiful, long hair in an attempt to stop the winged creature that darted over our heads. I ran out of the bathroom and headed toward the door.

Zoom! It darted closer this time. I was convinced…in the midst of someone's hair, is where that bat wanted to be!

The two of us huddled in two separate corners at the opposite ends of the cabin, and screamed mercilessly. My father arrived on the scene within minutes; he had heard us from the beach quite a distance away.

"A bat! A bat! It's after us!" I screamed.

My dad jumped into action. A slight man in build, but very agile and athletic, he grabbed a baseball bat and scaled the wall in mere seconds. He took position on the top of a beam in wait for the rodent with wings that was after his daughter.

As we cowered in wait of the extrication, my father pursued the enemy.

Within a matter of minutes, it was over. The bat was still and we were still. But my dad was visibly shaken. It was not fear, not for himself, but for us and, he was sorry about the bat.

Mary Amelia Paladin

My BatDad

The Adirondacks that are the Other Half of Me

"The Knotty Pine"

I was very small when we stayed in the Knotty Pine. It was a lovely cottage, made inside and out with a generous amount of knotty pine. It was built above the ground fifteen feet or so, which offered a filtered view of the lake.

We only stayed there once. It was the year I potty trained. Did I need to tell you that? No, I guess not, but it was one of my Adirondack milestones and it had to be included. An avid outdoors(wo)man in the Adirondacks makes the decision of time and location very carefully. It's no easy job.

Time and location is everything. My mother, coordinator of restroom policies and procedures, would have agreed. It wasn't easy keeping a toddler's pants dry when the door to the cottage is fifteen feet off the ground.

"The Hilltop"

We stayed in The Hilltop a few times in my 'tween years, that pleasant not child, yet not teen, stage of life. It was a pretty cottage of planed, natural pine planking which perched up on a little ridge overlooking two other cottages and the lake below.

A stone wall bordered its tiny front yard. It made a great place to play jacks, sunbathe, practice my handstands and read.

I heard a story about the building of this cottage, which was told to me by an elder family friend who has since passed away. He used to help the Meads on occasion with the construction of the cottages; this story was one of his favorites. It was about the construction of the wall.

The wall is (about) four feet tall. It's made of natural stone and concrete. The top of it is leveled with a thin layer of smooth cement. He told of Ruth, who was a petite woman, spreading the cement on top of the wall smoothly and precisely. It was in the 1950s and she was expecting their fourth child. She spread concrete on the far side of the top edge with one hand as she stretched forward and held her tummy up with her other one. She smoothed the cement evenly and she never needed help in doing so.

I see that wall every day in the summertime. I think back on the making of it, and the platform for fun it was for me and for many others as well.

It withstands time...still there, even though those who built it are gone.

"The Beachcomber"

The Beachcomber was a tiny cottage; it became one after its conversion from a small, beachside snack bar. It was one of the last cottages added to Mead's and we were one of the first families to stay in it. It was located only a few feet off the main stretch of beach on the lakefront.

It was a great location for a refreshment cabana. As a compact cottage with large windows and two passionate swimmers, it was less than great. It was imperative that we remain aware of the entire beach population, merely a windowpane away. To my dad, the man who never wore bathing trunks it was not an issue. To my mom and me, who, in one day changed bathing suits as often as most people open the refrigerator door, it was a constant embarrassment. We never burst into flames but more than once, we had to stop, drop, and roll.

"The Bay Pines"

This was, by far, the best cottage! We stayed in the Bay Pines for many, many years. Originally, we stayed there for our three weeks vacation, but by the last year that we rented it, we were staying the entire summer. It was a lovely cottage with a wonderful view of Brant Lake.

The knotty pine living room had a wall of six over six windows that allowed for a gorgeous breeze on a summer's night. Occcassionally a whiff of gasoline drifted in from the boat docks. To this day, the smell of gasoline triggers memories of summers on Brant Lake.

The small kitchen had a big, wood stove that threw off some serious heat. The shelves used for dishes and groceries didn't have doors. I had never seen that before and I thought it was quite rustic, a canvas for creativity. I arranged the items by color. Pretty, but not practical.

The screened-in porch was fabulous. The view and the breeze was a treat we savored every day.

Two bedrooms were in the rear of the cottage. My bedroom had twin beds and windows that were low to the ground. Perfect architectural placement for a teen to sneak out and meet friends on the beach. My mom, coordinator of stylish drapes and slipcovers, made the curtains. They were a vibrant mix of pinks, lime green, yellows and white. The pattern was, of course, psychedelic in design. It was the late 1960's, and those curtains were quite in vogue with the music of The Beatle's "Abbey Road" that blasted through the opened windows every day.

The bedroom in which my parents slept was off the kitchen and it was a smaller room with a double bed. My mom "hid" her purse under the window out of the sight of passers by but not me. However, when her cigarettes started to disappear, so did her purse.

***

The thing that I cannot describe adequately from memory though, is the feeling that I had all those summers that we stayed there.

There were sleepovers and sneak-outs, spaghetti-o cook offs, and grilled cheese and tomato sandwiches. Frequently, pots and pans covered the floors as the rain leaked in. Sandy water from our dripping bathing suits stuck to the bottom of our feet. Paper plates and plastic utensils left no dishes to wash. There were paperback books by the pile for my dad to read, or to prop up a bed if necessary. Numerous bathing suits, half of which belonged to others, hung on the clothesline. Wet colorful towels were draped everywhere to dry. As much sand was swept out of the cabin, as it seemed there was on the beach; swimming all day replaced our daily showers. Music mixed with laughter blasted from the windows. The floor shook as we danced until we were breathless.

So many wonderful times took place in that cottage. Happiness was bred and sheltered inside those walls. I am sure it did the same for many others before us, and, long after we moved on. For it was not the place that granted us our fond memories. It was the feeling that was realized in, and connected to, that little cottage tucked in the pines, in a little bay, on Brant Lake.

The Store
so much more than merchandise...

One of the most special, and infamous, things about Mead's Cottages was the store. I remember it so vividly that I can still see the arrangement of its wares and feel the relief of the cool air that enveloped me when I came in from the hot summer sun. I can even remember the little changes that occurred in merchandising throughout the years. Somewhat odd, but maybe my future as a retail business owner was working its way into my consciousness back then.

It was in the basement of the owners' home. It was a lovely home, yet not pretentious. Large, white and accented with (what I presume to be) local stone. It had a flagstone walkway made of different colored pieces and sizes, which stood back graciously on the green lawn waiting to welcome those who were coming to stay at Mead's for vacation. It was just as receptive to those who came solely to patronize the store.

The bustling mercantile hub was reached through the back lower level of the house. Years before handicap accessible requirements went into effect, the store was ready and able to be a place that anyone could enter, fulfill their needs, and enjoy the friendly atmosphere.

There was an area cleared of the dense trees where cars could pull in and park or fill their tanks at one of the two gas pumps. If not in use by cars, it was common to see boaters fill their fuel tanks at the pumps, load them into their trunks, onto wagons, or carry them by hand down the dirt road back to the waterfront.

An old, cast-off truck sat just a few feet into the woods. Those of us who were there for many years remembered it with fondness as we glanced its way. Most of us had ridden in it at one time or another. It had served its life well.

The store was probably quite typical of the region and era, but to us, *many* of us, it was far from typical.

The door to the store was wooden- not polished, planed or varnished- painted white and partially screened. It was framed within a large, screened-in porch of sorts, and it had a bell.

The bell…I can still hear it in my head along with the voices of children and customers as they paraded in and out. It rang all day and into the evening: seven, eight, nine, even (one year) ten o'clock, the entire summer. The **clang-clang** would sound each time the door slammed against its sturdy wooden frame.

Right inside the screened-in porch, on both sides of the door, was beer. *Lots* of beer. Six packs of all kinds were stacked from floor to ceiling. This proved to be a problem one year when the screens were sliced and quite a bit of that beer was taken. It then became an enclosed porch, with wooden sides.

One step up lifted you to the main level of the poured concrete floor. The step itself, however, was one giant piece of dark, gray rock. Local granite I would guess. Its top edge, worn smooth, bore a semi circular indentation made by the many feet that had trod upon it.

The Adirondacks that are the Other Half of Me

It was seldom quiet inside. Whether it was chatter, laughter, greetings or the quiet shared secrets of the children choosing penny candy, the store hummed with life.

There were fishermen. There were families. There were friends. There were travelers. They sought worms. They sought groceries. They sought conversation. It was available, all of it. It was plentiful and it was, unfortunately, taken for granted. The activity was constant; I guess we all thought it always would be. But of course, it would not.

Gone since the late 1970s is the brightly colored penny candy, the fishing worms stored behind the heavy snap doors in the bottom of the deli cooler, and the shelves of bread, rolls and coffeecakes. "Freddy Friehofer" (as we called the deliveryman) no longer travels on this side of the lake to drop off those magnificent chocolate chip cookies. We, the residents of the seasonal community, must go to town for our sundries. The days of "running to the store" for bread, milk, eggs, canned goods, breakfast stuff, or the evening's dessert are gone. Like so many other wonderful things, of a wonderful era, they have passed on.

I have told my daughter many stories about the store; of course, she can never truly understand its significance. She never knew the feeling of freedom, as a youngster alone, sent to the store on an errand for something. She never knew the hum of the store itself. She never knew the crackle of the electricity as it pulsated through the neon beer and soda signs. She never knew the potpourri of aromas that was made by groceries, candy, bait, produce, plastic swim toys and the gasoline pumps right outside.

The store at Mead's Cottages was extraordinary. It was not merely a place of commerce, at least not of the financial kind. Commerce I suppose it was; commerce of humanity. The exchanges of the lives, the loves, the sorrows and the happiness which were shared within it walls were priceless.

I can still hear the hum; I can still smell the smell; and I can still see the flashing neon. I can remember it all but none of my recollections will ever do justice to its importance in the lives of so many. Although I can remember all of that, as well as the slam of the door and the clang of the bell, I know I am not alone when I wish it were not just a memory.

"The Fire"
on the beach

That is what it was called…"The fire."

It was not called "the campfire" Nor "the bonfire". Not "the fire ring". Nor the "fire on the beach" (unless to inform someone new). It was all of that. But in our little world in the Adirondacks it was known as, "the fire".

It burned twenty-four hours a day, seven days a week, all summer long. I am not sure when, on what day, it was first lit each season although since Memorial Day seems to be the so-called official start of summer. Perhaps that was its annual inception.

A gigantic pile of split wood was stacked against the whole exterior wall of a nearby cottage; that pile was fuel for "the fire". Every year, some naive visitor made the remark that it would be impossible for all that wood to be used. Every year the skeptics were proven wrong. It was used in its entirety, and occasionally more had to be brought in to finish out the season.

But we, the summer regulars, knew better. There was never a doubt that the fire's flames would flicker. No doubt about the crackle of its fuel. No wrinkled brow as to why it burned. Whether it was a chilly August evening, or a hot, muggy, July afternoon, the fire burned.

Certainly it served its function well. Its purpose. Its call to employ. It toasted many marshmallows and cooked many hot dogs and ears of corn. It did all those things but it also did much more. To those of us that stayed at Mead's Cottages it was a given, a constant, a reality; the fire always burned.

We gathered there. We conspired there. We argued there. We discussed deep thoughts there. We fell in, and out of, love there. We were not unlike any other group of vacationers, (in any other vacation spot) that had a place, where it was only natural that people flocked.

Whether it was a crowded beach filled with families at a roast, or a huddled group of goose-bumped teenagers trying to warm up after a day full of waterskiing, the fire crackled. Whether it was a game of cards at the picnic table or a rainy day under the Shangri La, the fire endured. Whether it was a kiss under the stars after others had gone home, or the exchange of ideas and addresses as friends relished their time together, the fire danced in the center of our lives. Even as people came and went, even as they laughed and cried, and even as lives continued and passed, the fire burned brightly.

Often, I look toward that beach where the fire once burned. It is barren now, the remains of its existence, nearly gone. No longer does that brightness draw people to its side. No longer does it guide boats to shore at night. No longer does its undying flame reach toward the Adirondack sky that was once intoxicated by its wood smoke. Nevertheless, in my memory, as well as the memories of those who enjoyed its everlasting warmth the fire still crackles and dances in the hearts of our souls.

The Roasts
better than the celebrities'

Every week, all summer long, the entire cottage community descended upon the beach for either a hot dog roast (on Tuesdays) or, a corn roast (on Fridays).

They were held at night; the lake appeared to be a vast, darkened stage. The sky was pitch black, filled with millions of stars that sparkled like diamonds.

The beach was well lit by (what seemed like an endless) string of light bulbs that ran the full length of the waterfront. The beachfront was about 30-50 ft. from lakeside to its interior side, on which some of the cottages bordered.

On the northern end was the largest cottage of all, The Birches. It was two stories tall. The front of its lower level had huge screened windows that faced a beautiful expanse of the lake. The Shangri La, perched high off the sandy beach and had an open area below for multi-uses. Directly next door was The Beachcomber, a converted lakeside snack bar. A few yards southward was The Lake Shore, a medium sized cottage on a little rise with a screened in porch that overlooked the beach below. The Bay Pines was next to it across a sandy walkway; it was at the same elevation and was a sweet cottage. It overlooked the many small docks that were home to numerous boats of all types and sizes. The Green Trim was at the far southern end of the beach, nestled low into the trees it faced the wetlands and the paths that led from the campground area. Every cottage different, every cottage unique and every cottage brightly lit up inside as their lodgers enjoyed the festivities a few yards away.

In front of all of those cottages, on the main gathering area of the beach, a very large fire burned all the time, twenty-four hours, seven days a week, all summer long.

Around the fire, numerous Adirondack chairs in many colors were arranged and amongst those was a variety of other types. Many chairs were needed on roast night, and in every one of those chairs were very happy families! In July, they were dressed in lighter weight summer garb with perhaps a sweatshirt. But by the end of August, everyone donned long pants, layers of sweaters and jackets on top. The sandals and flip-flops of July were replaced by socks and sneakers or hiking boots in August. There were even times when a set of gloves or mittens appeared!

Some of the cottage and camp moms helped serve the food at the gigantic picnic table. In preparation, they pushed a huge tube of white paper, unrolled it down the length of the table to cover its rough surface. They set up the condiments and the paper supplies then formed a production line. They were darn good at what they did. They passed out hot dogs that had been cooked over the open fire, or corn on the cob that had been boiled in a giant kettle over the fire to each person who wanted one. They saw to it that everyone had at least one serving before allowing any young campers to belly up for seconds!

The dads assisted in the cooking. Every Tuesday night they held the hotdog cages in the fire, their hands reddened and their faces wrinkled up from the scorching heat.

The cages held so many hot dogs that they had to prop them on logs for support until they were done. On Friday nights a huge galvanized tub of water was threaded onto a long metal pole that hung above the blaze. Dozens of ears of sweet corn were cooked in the bubbling water as the men watched carefully. When it was done, they carried it to the table and pulled the steaming, sun-yellow corn out of the salted brew. The ears of corn were stacked high until they were dunked in a big steel pan filled with sweet, creamy, melted butter.

Close to the table, under the eave below the Shangri-La, was an old, red Coca Cola machine. It had not worked automatically for some time that I can remember, but on roast nights it was filled with cases and cases of a variety of sodas. They filled the machine (the refrigeration worked) and everyone selected the flavor of choice. I loved Coke, my mom loved grape Nehi and my dad loved Schaeffer. He did not get that from the red machine.

After food and drinks were had by all, the grownups sat around the fire for hours. Kids played until they were exhausted; they were great nights and bedtime was always delayed.

There was an old upright piano on the beach underneath a small wooden shelter; it came alive on roast nights. One of the seasonal guests played "Shine on Harvest Moon", "Rubber Tree Plant", "Mack the Knife", "Mr. Sandman" and other songs of the time. The bunny hop was a big favorite and children joined the adults for that one regularly; the line reached (at least) 40-50 people long. The laughter and songs floated out over the lake and danced on its surface before ascending into the nighttime air, then disappearing into the starlit sky.

A sing along on roast night

During the roasts, children played games; they did not need toys, or boards. They needed only their bodies and imaginations.

The game Blacksmith was one of the games. It required everyone to run like wild Indians throughout the entire cottage community. It was a big favorite. It was similar to hide and seek but no one stayed in one place, and a flashlight was used to "tag" the person. One had to be able to run like the wind. If they were spotted they had to run back to safety on the beach before the person who was "it" got there. Short cuts were always allowed and those of us that knew all the short cuts left the new kids in the dust.

Buck-Buck, was a much different kind of game. The "anchor", usually one of the bigger, older kids, put their arms around a big tree. The Buck-Buck Tree, as it was known, was a very tall, very old, maple tree. It also had boat propellers, of many assorted sizes nailed to it, on display ten feet or so off the ground. How none of them ever fell on the head of a Buck-Buck(er) is a question I wonder about to this day.

The next player on the team bent over, wrapped their arms around the anchor's waist, and then tucked their head between their own arm and the anchor's waist. It formed like this until all team members were in alignment and formed one long platform with their backs. The opposing team vaulted one by one leapfrog style, onto the backs of the tree huggers until all members were on top of their platform of backs. Some vaulted all the way up to the tree. Some hung upside down, some had their own teammates on top of them. When the last jumper had landed, "Buck-Buck!" resonated loud and strong. All those on board, wiggled, bounced, giddy-upped and carried on until the tree hugging team collapsed.

When I was young I could not vault far, or high. I was not an asset to the team and I was always picked and sent last; sometimes I even fell on my own with out even being bucked. I was never any good at the game but I played anyway. By the time I hit thirteen I could vault up and over much more easily. I was absolutely thrilled the first time I vaulted far enough up the line to slam my forehead on the Buck-Buck tree.

When eleven o'clock came, the younger children were sent back to their cottages and camps with older siblings to care for them. The adults would continue to socialize, sing and laugh.

There was no vulgarity. There were no things done in poor taste. There were no unpleasant moments.

There was always friendship. There was always consideration. There was always respect.

As I reflect back and compare that world to the one of today, my consolation is...There is always tomorrow, and there is always hope.

The Old Upright
spoke to us in song

The dark brown piano sat in the same place for many years on our beach. It was embraced between two tall trees; a little peaked roof with a bit of tarpaper protected it from the weather. It was a stable reminder of voices, faces, and lives that once were…Not a reminder that made one melancholy, a reminder of the happiness, laughter and friendship that had gathered around it. It played an important role for so many years. Simple years. Years when contentment came from sharing time, sharing place.

Through the decades, the old upright had sounded out the cadence to "The Bunny Hop". It had soothed the dark evening's chill with "Shine on Harvest Moon". It had made clusters of children laugh with "Rubber Tree Plant". It was tall, it was proud, and it performed its job superbly. It did not matter who was at the keyboard; it did not matter if it was finely tuned. It only mattered that it sang- so we could.

I remember it being at its post when I was quite small and it stood at attention for many years. Eventually it grew tired and weakened yet, it always played when called upon. Perhaps it did not have the strength it once had; perhaps its voice had faded, but it always managed to muster enough power to bring a song from those around it.

The last time I listened to it was well into the 1970s. The old piano, although protected from the elements, could not be protected from the passage of time. Its veneer was well worn and chipped; some of the keys had lost their once white armour, those that retained it, were cracked and curled.

A group of us sat on the beach on a wet and dreary, summer afternoon. We were quiet, almost glum, something that seldom happened in our circle of friends. One of the boys sat down on the low, tiny, round stool- no longer adjustable- crippled by the years. He played "Low Spark of High Heeled Boys" and "Color My World".

The songs made us smile. We gathered around the piano as we had since we were little, and we sang songs of our generation. A generation that saw the end of the proud upright and its music. It had, for such a long time, colored our world and that of many others.

The Garbage Truck
a.k.a Wheeled Meals

It was a big thrill to watch the raccoons, and occasionally bears, help themselves to a late night snack, courtesy of the vacationers who stayed at Mead's Cottages. An old pickup truck with high wooden sides was used for the collection of trash. It was driven weekly to the local dump for disposal. But the days in between afforded a smorgasbord of delight for the nocturnal feeders that lived nearby.

First, listening was required. Then the determination if the diners were raccoons, or bears. Raccoons posed no threat but a mama bear with cubs was a very different story; extra caution was a must!

Everyone knew, that if snuck upon very quietly, without any flashlights lit, chances were very good that digging, munching, critters would be seen. When it was confirmed that there were critters feasting, one flashlight was illuminated. The animals did not seem to mind that. But when multiple lights blazed, the creatures ran away.

I saw a mama bear once; she was inside the truck bed, scavaging through the bags of trash. We had the flashlight on her as we watched quietly. We heard a few little whimper-like sounds, and sure enough…two babies were in a tree nearby. When we realized they were there, we backed up quite a distance to oberve from afar. The babies were about ten feet off the ground in the branches of a big tree on the far side of the truck. Fortunately, we were not positioned between mama and her babies; apparently she felt we were not a threat as long as we kept a respectable distance. She continued to rummage for a few minutes more then made a soft grumble and the babies began to scamper down the tree. While they climbed down, she climbed out of the truck. They met on the ground and she coaxed them forward into the woods. They quietly dissappeared into the darkness and they were gone. It was as if they had never been there at all.

Another time I saw two young adults. They were midsized, not nearly as big as the mama bear had been,. Their coats were beautiful; very shiny and almost a blue-black in color. When the flashlight caught their fur in just the right manner, it seemed to reflect light like a multi-faceted gem. Their dark eyes looked back at us as bright green from the glare of the light and their black noses shone from the moisture of their breath. It was possible to hear an occasional snort, unless of course cornhusks, soup cans, or potato chip bags covered their noses!

Raccoons were entirely different; once the light shone on them and their initial caution subsided, multiple lights could blast fervently; it was almost as if they enjoyed the attention. They dug and wrestled, and chased and played with each other amongst the piles of trash. Raccoons love marshmallows, and discards of campfire s'mores were always plentiful. Bags with a few of the sweet candy pillows or wrappers from chocolate bars were a much desired commodity to the clumsy characters.

Mama raccoon was not aggressive as long as a sensible distance was kept by all onlookers. The babies were adorable; round balls of fur, with huge, dark eyes and ringed tails. Their masked faces popped up here and there; as though they performed just for us. The mini bandits frolicked and fell head first into the mountains of trash. They chattered to each other, and their mother, as they made fun out of serious work.

For those cute garbage pickers, the night before haul away day was a feast beyond compare!

Pancakes sans Milk
shortcut sans end

My poor dad. He was hampered throughout his entire life by the lack of a homing device with which most of us seem to be born.

The North Country misadventures became stories that preceded my father at every turn. His adventures were always a good topic at parties, campfires and family gatherings. My parents' entire group of friends knew of his shortfall and kept an eye on him. My dad was, by no means, careless or foolish. He just got lost easily.

He always had the best of intentions. He was not afraid to venture off , whether it was in a car, train, bus, or on foot. He always started out as though he were different than he truly was…navigationally challenged.

My father was a very practical and pensive man. He seldom took chances on things that could end badly. So as I look back it makes me wrinkle a brow. My dad…the rock of our lives, the protector from all scary things, the voice of infallible common sense and reason, took some chances when he put himself in the pilot's seat. My dad was also a very optimistic man; he was happy, funny, and full of life. When I think of that trait, I realize why he was able to forge onward as though each time would be different. Better. Successful.

One Saturday morning, while at Brant Lake, my mother sent my father to the general store on site. We had run out of milk and she was making pancakes for breakfast. She had the ingredients to make the pancakes, but we needed the milk to drink with them.

My uncle's camp, where we stayed, was less than one hundred yards away from the store- through the woods. From the many years of people cutting through the woods as a short cut to the store. It led right to the clearing near its door.

My mom asked my dad to hurry. The pancakes were fresh; to keep them that way, she stacked them on a hot-plate.

My dad walked out the door.

He returned two and a half hours later. And he did not have any milk.

On that short path, my dad somehow lost notice of the trodden ground and walked all over the woods throughout the cottage area. He could hear the bell on the store's door clang; he tried to walk toward it. He knew when he had gone too far in the wrong direction, because the sound of the bell became less audible. He knew when he was near the main road, because he could hear the cars through the trees.

My dad did not find the store, but he did find his way back to camp. We were all pleased about *that*.

Despite the lack of milk, we ate our pancakes, which were more than cool by then. My dad told us all about his adventure. We laughed together and shook our heads; it had happened again; my poor father had gotten lost.

After breakfast, my dad asked me if I would accompany him to the store. He remarked that the pancakes tasted great, but we really should have milk in the camp anyway.

The Adirondacks that are the Other Half of Me

Even at six years old, I knew it was not about the milk. It was about a lesson in forest navigation.

Bears, Bible and a Boy
a visit home

In 1962, there was an elderly man who stayed at Mead's Cottages; my mom took me to meet him one evening. She told me he was someone special. His name was Jesse David Roberts and he had written a book, a book about his life growing up at Brant Lake. My mother had already met him earlier in the day; she had struck up a conversation with him while walking past his cottage.

As I mentioned earlier, my mom genuinely loved people. She would strike up a conversation with anyone, anywhere, any time. She was sincere in her interest in what they had to say and she could (and would) talk about any topic.

Mr. Roberts stayed in the Martha Ray; the reason his cabin residency made an impression on my seven-year-old brain was that there had recently been a surfeit of baby skunks under that cabin. The mama skunk had sprayed the collie that stayed in The Birches, next door. The owners of that unfortunate canine had to bathe her in (what seemed like) ten thousand gallons of tomato juice. I wondered if Mr. Roberts knew that. I wondered if he had heard and/or smelled them at night. Most likely, when he went to bed, they woke up. I also wondered if he had a dog.

He was a lovely man, in his eighties at the time although he did not seem old. He *looked* very old to my eyes, but his voice and spirit seemed very young. He was a thin man with a white beard. I noted that it was not a Santa Claus type of beard, the wide kind that rests on an expansive chest but does not seem to move when the person talks. It was a short, narrow beard that hung straight, free of his chest and neck; it bobbed up and down slowly each time he spoke. I recognized much later, that it was because he was tall and his face thin that his whiskers were able to move along with his jaw. He was very pleasant and seemed interested in speaking with me. He obviously loved sharing his childhood memories of Brant Lake. I loved hearing them. He knew the settlers of many years ago; he himself lived near the very spot on which we stood that very moment!

His book, "Bears, Bible and a Boy-Memories of the Adirondacks" is a wonderful book. It is the story of his family: his father, his mother and the nine children that made up the Roberts family. He tells of the bears that his father pursued, the dogs that ran by his side, the hardships (that he didn't mind), the family that was close-knit with a true devotion to God. The book begins when Mr. Roberts was four years old. It continues through the sale of the family farm at the northern end of Brant Lake to the passing of his beloved father. The book is out of print now but if you are fortunate enough to find a copy, please read this story of life in the North Country. Life that was hard yet its rewards many. It is an inspiring read for devotees of Adirondack life…

A True Camper
I am not

My very first overnight camping trip was into Pharaoh Lake when I was eight. I remember my age at the time of that adventure because I remember almost every moment of it. Every anxiety filled moment of it….

My friend's father decided to take a group of us on an overnight campout. He was a strict and unpleasant man. He was also a Boy Scout leader who thought of himself as a leader of little soldiers. I would have begged my mother to deny my request to go had I been old enough to understand his personality. The fact that he woke his children to Reveille every morning may have been a red flag to someone more grown up than I was.

The trip started poorly. Our leader checked our packs and made us repack them until they were done to the specifications he thought necessary. His children had done well, one of the boys had done well, but another boy and I had not.

Apparently, my inexperience as the perfect camper became obvious quite early into the adventure. It was brought to everyone's attention that a unicorn sleeping bag was a ridiculous choice and very inappropriate for camping. I am sure that my mother didn't expect such scrutiny when she purchased it for my birthday a few weeks earlier. What she did expect was that I would love the regal, white unicorn that frolicked on a background of aqua, purple and fuchsia, (my favorite colors at the time).

I didn't have the proper insect repellent, socks, or sneakers for hiking. It wasn't wise that I had packed peanut butter and homemade strawberry jam sandwiches because the sweetness was like a dinner bell to raccoons. I didn't like cold cuts, and despite my mother's plea to take some with me, she made me three PB&J sandwiches and Hershey's chocolate milk in a Three Stooges thermos- *yikes*. The evidence to prove my camping deficit grew.

During most of the hike into the lake, I was last in line. The bugs were getting snarled in my ringlets and the mosquitoes were transfusing on my neck. My fear of snakes was clearly my most annoying concern. But I had seen two before we ever crossed the footbridge at the trailhead. I considered that a bad omen. I was scared.

One of my friends recognized that I was out of my element; he hung back and kept my spirits up. It felt great to know that someone would notice if I became trail mix to a nest of poisonous snakes. Just the fact that there was a "someone" was wonderful; the fact that I had a very big crush on him almost made the trip bearable.

We reached lakeside in three hours, just around dinnertime. It was the longest three hours of the eight years I had spent on earth.

There are lean-tos at Pharaoh Lake, but they were all occupied. That meant my shelter for the night would be the wild black yonder.

We set up camp. We dug a small hole a short distance away (for you know what). We built a fire and we put on a pot of Spaghetti Os. We collected sticks for marshmallows.

The Adirondacks that are the Other Half of Me

We gathered water to rinse our dishes and ourselves. Then, we hung all the food in a tree.

Next we set up our sleeping arrangement: side by side in a straight line, parallel to the shoreline (seriously). My friend's dad had decided that, since it was my first campout, I needed to sleep on one of the ends to overcome my fears.

I protested a bit but, the more I voiced my reservations, the more he insisted that I conform. He was not a man with whom one argued. So I surrendered. I was beaten. I was angry. And I was really scared. The hours that continued between set up and lights out, were anxious ones for me. I could not enjoy the ghost stories, the marshmallows, or the popcorn. I wanted it to be morning; I wanted to go home.

I lay in my brightly colored sleeping bag and looked up; I clenched the top around and underneath my quivering chin. It was cold, I think, or maybe I was just so scared that my teeth chattered. The food bag hung closely to my left, about ten feet off the ground. I stared at the huge bag of bear bait. I envisioned a grizzly as it hung from it, shredding everything in its sight in an attempt to gain access to the food. Everything, including the nearest person. *That* would be me...

The fire was dying and the dark was getting blacker. I knew I would not be sleeping that night. All I hoped for, by that point, was that the giant grizzlies would take the food and run. My eyes were locked on the looming bundle above me. I swore it was coming to life.

Once the fire had gone out completely, I felt a tap on my shoulder.

"Here, trade places." It was the voice of my friend, my crush, my hero.

He took my hand and helped me crawl from under the watchful eye of my trusty unicorn. He had his sleeping bag in his hand, ready to flop it in my spot and flip mine to his.

Silently, my friend swapped the bags and crawled into his which was now on the dreadful end. He didn't help me into mine. He didn't say anything. And he didn't make me feel like a baby.

I looked up. The ominous bag hanging in the tree stopped moving, the wild animals were satiated and the black yonder didn't look so wild. I closed my eyes and said a silent thank you to my friend- who had just become so much more important to me than a "crush".

Swamp Thing
it made my conscience sing

It was a beautiful morning, very early on a quiet Sunday in late July. My dad had left for Mass and my mom was still asleep.

I was not allowed near the water without an adult. Even though I was a good swimmer by then, my mom and dad were very responsible parents and they *never* took chances with me.

My friend and I were playing out on the screened porch when my dad left. I was told not to go anywhere until my mom got up so, of course, I would never have thought to do otherwise.

My friend, however, couldn't wait until my dad was out of earshot. "Let's go get some peepers," she said. Her eyes were wide with the idea and she began to stand up.

"I can't, my mom isn't up yet," said I, the obedient one.

"So?" she said. Her eyes now looked at me as if I had twelve heads. "We can be back before she even wakes up. Who will know?"

"I don't think I'd better." I shook my head slightly.

"Fine. I'll go and get someone else to come with me." She headed toward the cabin door.

To an only child, the threat of being replaced by another friend, foe, or anything in between, is like being sentenced to a future of unbearable solitude. The unknown activities, produced by not being included, would absolutely crush me. That is how secrets started, tales are told (granted, not always true ones) and best friends are made, or lost. I could not take that chance.

"Well, we'll have to be really quick. I don't want to get in trouble." My stomach was twisting into knots.

One thing I already knew at that early age was, that I could get away with *nothing*. Somehow, my mom always found out when I did something wrong. I never understood how that happened, but it always did. I do not have any idea why I thought the peeper capture would go off without a hitch. I did know that I was not going to be the one left behind or worse yet, replaced if I did not go.

We each grabbed a pail and headed toward the swamp.

The swamp still exists, but it is not very large anymore. It was partially filled in many years ago and is only a fraction of the size it once was. Large or small, it was never a place that I enjoyed.

I did not tell any of my friends that I was leery of the muck, or the things that lived in it. I knew if I told them they would make fun of me. If they knew how absolutely terrified of snakes I was, I knew one would magically appear in my face, on my feet, in my towel or somewhere else way too close to me. So, I sucked it up.

The swamp loomed in front of us. It was getting hot and the humidity was thick. The steam was coming up from the muck like a grade B horror movie. I almost expected some green-gilled creepy thing to be submerged amongst the cattails, its black eyes watching us as we planned our siege on the peepers. My eyes combed the surface thoroughly, constantly in search of 'something'. But I saw nothing.

The Adirondacks that are the Other Half of Me

Peepers are the teeny little frogs that make sounds at night as if they are calling "peep…peep…peep…" Their chorus is loud and truly indicative of summer. I always thought they were adorable and they were plentiful in the swamp. They were very easy to catch.

We filled the bottom of our pails with small stones and pulled some swamp grass. We added it to the plastic sand buckets that were to be the habitat for the little creatures. We would let them go a few hours later. We never intended to treat them poorly; we just wanted to watch and study their behavior. Surprisingly to us, they never touched the swamp grass that we thought should look so deliciously enticing to a peeper.

We caught a dozen or so each and then decided to head back to my camp. We could watch them and then leave the pails on the side of the cabin in the shade, so my mom didn't see them. We would return the tiny frogs to their colony after lunch.

"rrrebbit…rrrebbit…"

It was so loud that we were startled for a moment. We scanned the swamp for the origin of the bellow. There, about six feet from the shoreline, was a huge bullfrog. It had those giant black eyes, that I knew I had felt, watching us; it was resting on the surface of the swamp among the cattails and willowy reeds. The eyes in my manifestation had been, however, in the face of a huge, green swamp monster or a mutant, muck slithering, serpent.

"Let's get him!" my friend said.

What?!?!?!

My heart skipped a beat.

"How? He is pretty far out." I said. The thought of getting back to camp had taken flight and was shared with the thought of this conquest.

We looked around and spotted an old piece of planking, discarded from a dock's construction. It was partially submerged at the edge of the muck.

"Hey! There! Let's try that." She ran over, grabbed it and walking backwards, dragged it to the edge of the muck near where the frog had perched.

"If I can get it to stay out over the muck, I can walk out on it and grab him." She was almost breathless.

I was almost breathless, but for a different reason…

Certainly she must be nuts! Why in the world would anyone want to balance over that muck?

It was like quicksand. How could she know what was slithering, crawling, sucking or biting beneath the surface? She was crazy, I was confident of that.

I watched and shook my head as she slowly balanced her way out the length of the slimy, rotted piece of wood.

No way. Oh, noooo way.

My friend was very tiny. She was two years older than I was, but she was petite. She had beautiful, long brown hair, which on that morning was braided and hung down her back nearly to her waist. Her legs were muscular and toned from years of ballet. She was as agile as a sprite.

She leaned down but, try as she did, her arms were just too short to reach the bullfrog.

"I can't quite reach him!" She was frustrated and sweating. She stretched farther and wobbled a bit. "Whoa!" she exclaimed.

"Forget him; we'll see if he comes in closer later today, when we bring the peepers back." I picked up my pail and waited.

"No, I want him." she said.

I knew this was not going to end soon or well.

"I've got to go back to camp. Are you coming?"

"Wait, c'mere." she said. She stood up and quickly, but daintily, retraced her steps and hopped back onto the shore.

"You are taller. You can probably reach him." Her eyes on me, I could tell that she fully expected me to oblige.

"I don't know about that. I'm not walking out over that muck." I shook my head in an attempt to be firm.

My friend liked control; she did not like it if she did not get her way.

"Geeze, come on. What are you afraid of?" Her lip curled up to one side.

I knew I was in trouble. "Nothing. I just have to get home."

"Oh, okay." She gave me a look I recognized. I knew what was coming next, "I'll go find someone to get him. Never mind..." she turned slightly and paused.

"Wait. All right. But I need to hurry." I laid my pail down.

She smiled in victory.

She stepped aside.

So, out on the rotted board I ventured...I took much smaller steps than she did. I felt the board sink a bit, so I paused. I had expected to sink a little; I knew I weighed more than she did. I gathered my thoughts and planned my next step, then the next. So far, so good. Another...then a half step. I stopped. I waited. No movement. Good. I was at the end of the board.

The shiny, bullfrog blinked up at me. He made no movement to escape; I guess he knew there would be no need, because the moment I saw him blink at me for the second time, the board gave way and down I went!

My heart pushed upward into my throat as though the swamp muck was squeezing it up through my body. I began to feel the cool, thick mud take claim to my shoes, legs, then clothes. My arms remained free and I was waving them rapidly.

"Help! Help me!"

I could not turn around to see her. My body was a prisoner of the rancid smelling goo and I felt as though I was still sinking. I was not; but in my mind's eye, it was merely a matter of time before I disappeared completely into the slimy grave that was to be my punishment for being where I should not have been. Imagination took charge. Instead of the bullfrog in front of me, I saw an endless, slithering parade of the dreaded Water Moccasins which, according to my friends, were said to be in abundance in the swamp. They were gliding toward me, their devilish forked tongues and venom-dripping fangs, salivating for my flesh.

"I can't. I can't lift you. I'll get help."

I should have been offended, because she meant it exactly the way it came out. But I, at that moment, didn't care.

"Don't leave me here alone. The snakes, what about the snakes?!?!"

But she was gone. I was alone. Just me and the bull-frog and the Water Moccasins, and the leeches, and the quicksand-like muck.

I, am a goner…

I prayed I could survive to endure my parents' disappointment at my trickery. I deserved it, and at that moment, I longed for it. I was sure I was not going to live through this escapade.

The terror continued to surge through my body for what seemed like an hour. It was, in fact, less than ten minutes. The stink turned my stomach and I was glad that I had not yet eaten breakfast. Cocoa Krispies would not have smelled good mixed with swamp crud and snake venom.

I heard footsteps coming through the path. I could tell some were my friend's, fast and light. I knew the other ones were that of an adult. They were heavier and slower.

"Oh, Dolly…" I heard the deep voice come from behind.

A familiar voice; it was my uncle. My heart leapt.

Hooray! He will fix this mess.

My uncle's camp was across from my friend's; she had gotten him to come back with her. My dad's brother was quite tall. He had no problem stretching out to reach my exposed arm. With one strong pull he yanked me out of the muck.

He was, like my dad, a man of few words. For a moment, I was not sure whether to be happy, or cry. Either way, I was out of that infernal prison and anything that came my way was small in comparison.

He looked at me, squarely in the eyes. "What are you doing down here, Dolly?"

He called me that often; I thought it was a pet name, but fifty-plus years later, I learned that it seems to be a somewhat common expression of familiarity in my paternal family's hometown of Albany. Still, whenever I hear someone use it, I think of my uncle.

"I was trying to get that bullfrog out there." I pointed to a spot that was now empty. "Well, he was there."

"Where's your father?" he asked.

"At Mass and mom's asleep." The morning sun was growing stronger and I squinted as I looked up at him.

"Well Dolly, I think you had better get back up to your camp before your mom wakes up." He eyes still looked into mine.

"Yes, I think so too." I glanced sourly at my friend, "We have been gone way too long and I am going to get in trouble anyway for coming down here. I don't want her to worry if she wakes up."

"Good idea," he smiled. "Do I need to talk to your father?"

"No, I'll tell him. My mom will probably know, even before I tell her anyway."

My uncle chuckled, "Yes, she does have her ways of discovery doesn't she?"

He tousled my curly hair and pulled a broken piece of reed from it. "Go on now…"

"Bye." I said hesitantly. "Thanks, Uncle Jake."

"Go now." He said quickly.

He and my aunt never had children and I could tell there were times he didn't quite know what to say to me. That was one of them.

He turned and headed in the direction of his camp.

My friend and I slowly started back to my camp; I was smelly, sticky, itchy, and totally uncomfortable. I was ashamed of myself and I was a bit mad at her. She, for once, was speechless.

We reached the crest of the path and I looked up toward my camp. Since the day had started out so poorly, I truly expected to see my mother on the porch. However, she was not.

My friend started to follow me into the camp but I stopped her. "I'll see you later."

"You aren't going to tell her, are you?" she asked, visibly in disbelief.

"Yes, I am. She'll find out anyway so I may as well do it first."

She shook her head, "Okay, it's your life." She turned and walked out.

I knocked on my parents' bedroom door and called to her as I entered, "hey Mom, I just saw Uncle Jake. He was down by the swamp and guess what…"

I acted as happy. I thought if I enhanced it a bit it might work in my favor.

"He pulled me out just before I got sucked under."

My mom sat up in bed and looked at me; her eyes did not look the least bit sleepy.

The coordinator of detection already knew.

Everybody in the Water
an unexpected 'dip'

The beach was crowded with campers that came to see the fireworks scheduled for the evening. It was going to be an exciting evening. We had no idea exactly how exciting it would become.

It was dusk and we watched the four men in the boat row the distance to the swimming float. Once they got there, they slowly unloaded the boat of its cargo.

Cases of fireworks (this was the early 1960s) were delicately placed on the float. The boat was tied to the opposite side and a large metal tub was eased into the water, filled, and carried to a place next to the wooden cases.

Time passed; we watched as the men prepared the area and safely organized everything for ignition of the display of lights.

As dark settled, the preparations were finished; the men had waited for complete darkness to begin. We could hear bits and pieces of their conversations as they checked and double-checked the area. We could no longer see their silhouettes. Only the light and movement of their flashlights gave way to any indication of their positions.

Then we saw a match ignite; we knew it was time to begin and everyone was silent with anticipation. The first bit of propelled, colored light seared the sky and exploded into a million tiny flashes of brilliance. Then the next one and another. The rest ensued. Each one as beautiful as the last. The ooohs, and aaahs were a stream of auditory delight as adults applauded and children squealed. The activity continued for a generous amount of time.

A pause in the display led us to believe that the end was nearing; everyone began to move around in their chairs a bit. No one got up to leave just in case there were more to come. It was apparent that the men were cleaning up or gathering the debris. Once we were able to see them rowing nearer shore, we would know that it was finished.

All of a sudden we saw a spark. We heard a man's yell and we saw a flash. Silhouetted, in the split second of the flash, we were able to see the four men jump off the float in all directions. We then saw light. Lots of light. Many colored, spasmodic lights flew everywhere. Much more illumination at once than we had seen earlier in the display. Everyone was hushed as we watched in worry. Fortunately, it lasted less than a minute and all was quiet.

The lack of any sound was deafening to us; we considered the worst. We did not hear a thing, nor could we see anything. After a panic-stricken moment or two, someone jumped from his chair and ran toward the water. He was about to swim to the float when a man's voice came from the shoreline. It was one of the four men from the float. They had already made it to shore; he assured us they were fine.

As the years faded, the horror that could have resulted and the recollections became more humorous. It turned out to be legendary. The story of the fireworks on the float often got top billing around the fire. The memory of the four men, silhouettes distinguished by the explosions all around them, grew more and more colorful. It was a favorite to everyone, even those men who took that unexpected swim.

Waterski? Piece of cake
er…lake

These days, wakeboarding seems to be the number one water sport; but in my youth it was waterskiing. Anyone who was worth their weight in salt, and stayed on a lake in the Adirondacks, had to know how to waterski. The better you were at it…the better you were!

The first time I tried, I was seven years old. I had learned to swim very early, so neither my mother nor I had any reservations about my learning the sport. The thought of it was exhilarating to me; I could hardly wait!

Waterskiing lessons were frequent and ample. All one had to do was be out on the dock when the boat came in to tow. Often ski time went from early morning until late afternoon.

When my turn came, I could hardly contain myself. It looked like so much fun! I went to the edge of the dock and waited for my directions; a young camper, my senior by a few years, was next to me. He assisted the boat driver and spotter. He stayed at my side. They instructed as he guided me.

He showed me how to step into and adjust the ski boots and told me to lock them into the position that held my feet securely.

Securely? I already felt the circulation in my feet being choked at the ankles!

Next, I had to sit down on the dock, which was much easier said than done.

My two feet were prisoners in suction cupped one by six planks and I had to try to fit my bum (my Scottish mother's nice term for, well, you know what) in between them and sit down. At seven, I did not worry much about finesse. But I did wonder how the heck I would not lose my balance and break my, soon to be, splinter-riddled bum!

Had I been a ballerina, and not a tomboy at that age, I may have figured it out a bit more easily and gracefully. But, I was not, and I did not.

Plop! I went down. It hurt; it was not pretty, but I made it and, I had not gotten any splinters in the process.

Next, I had to wiggle myself off the edge of the dock and into the water. I saw this as another harrowing opportunity to be pierced by the ragged, lead-laced daggers of wood. I had had many 'slivers' already by that age, and they hurt alot. My mom was not the coordinator of delicate splinter removal; my dad was better at it but he was not due at camp for another week.

So, with a foam life belt around the waist of my red tartan, one piece bathing suit, I slid into the water with gusto.

I bobbed around like a weeble as I tried to get the waterskis under control. They had come alive and were taking off in opposite directions, leaving me to thrash my arms like propellers as I tried to corral them back with legs that no longer belonged to me.

"Keep the rope between the skis, keep the tips out of the water and together, arms straight. Don't bend them, or lean back, when you feel the boat pull!" Those were my instructions, shouted from the boat that rocked in various directions as the driver turned the wheel to straighten it out.

Okay. I'll try...

I was pretty sure I could do that, if my head did not lean to the side when my entire body floated sideways from the momentum of the skis toppling. Perhaps if I was not holding onto a rope that was floating around the ski tips like a spider web in the wind, things would improve. By the time I got one thing together, the other two fell apart.

Oh, boy...I hope I can do this.

Swimming had been a heck of a lot easier to learn and a lot more fun. I only had myself to control, not five other variables. Of course at that age I did not know they were variables, but I did know that things were not going well.

The driver turned around to look at us; the spotter had not stopped looking at us despite the absolute embarrassment I had come to feel. And my helper was coaxing me on.

I squeezed the wooden handle of the ski rope with hands that were at the end of two rigidly locked arms. Eyes fixed forward on the ski tips with the rope in between, I said quietly to the boy, "Okay."

His hand shot out of the water, his thumb pointed upward and that was the last thing I saw.

The force of the boat's pull yanked me not only out of the water, but also out of the decorative planks that had been affixed to my feet. My body flew up, then down, head first into the water that now felt like a brick wall. When I surfaced, the handle of the ski rope, which had been ripped from my hands, slapped across the surface of the roiling water as the boat circled back toward me and my new instructor friend.

Whack! Whack! Whack! The boat swung around and headed straight at us. Then, Slosh! the driver cut the acceleration; it smoothly glided next to us.

"Try again?" I heard the driver yell.

"Sure!" I yelled back.

What?!?!? What the heck was I thinking!?!?!?

I closed my eyes, dropped my head backwards into the water, and shook it.

You can do this…

Getting the skis back on my feet while in the water was a thousand times harder than on the dock. It took what seemed like hours. I bobbed. I twisted. I went belly up. I went bum up. I went every which way until I finally got the skis onto my feet. Kindly, my helper had held onto the rope until I got situated. I would not have been able to snag that undulating piece of apparatus as well!

Okay, I've got it now…This is it.

Many other kids my age could already ski. I had to do it.

I looked over at my helper. He smiled and handed me the rope. I wobbled a bit and floated around from the waves, but I propelled myself back to position.

Arms locked, I yelled "Okay!"

Success would be mine…

Camper Boy's thumb went up. The motor sounded, the pull came, I felt the jerk, and then…

Oooooooooooowwwwwwwwwww!

A very sharp pain creased the side of my neck. Panic erupted. I let go. I went under, I sucked in water, and then let myself go limp. I knew the air in my lungs (and the life belt) would float me to the surface. My mother had taught me that when she taught me to swim.

When I did surface, my hand went to my neck. The welt had already started to erupt and there was blood on my shaking hand.

The ski rope had had too much slack in it when I signaled ready. I did not know that I was not ready. It had whirred past my neck as the slack drew tight, giving me a good rope burn. Nevertheless, it scared me enough to call it quits.

It was not the fault of anyone. It was not even serious. But it delayed my learning to waterski until the ripe old age of fourteen. Late, for a "lake kid".

Nearing day's end of water skiing

Mary Amelia Paladin

I must end this by telling you that once I did learn to waterski I became passionate about it; I became well worth my weight in salt. I loved it and usually skied through October, until the age of 31 when I had my daughter and became the stoddegty old worrywart that I now am.

There is nothing more exhilarating than the reflection of the blue sky beneath you as you soar across water that returns visions like a mirror made of dark glass. It appears rigid, yet it allows you to glide over its silken surface. The feeling bathes you in the warmth of the sun, the chill of the autumn air and the spray of the glorious clean water.

All that and so much more, amidst the fragrance of pine and wood smoke.

Rite of Passage
was habit forming

I thought I'd follow the waterskiing adventure with this story because, you see, when one made it up on waterskis (or had a birthday) there was a rite of passage.

You already read about the roasts that were held on our beach every Tuesday and Friday evenings. Yes, there was campfire cooking; there was eating and drinking and singing too. There were children playing, and there was dancing and laughing as well. There was also a certain rite of passage and that…was being thrown into the lake.

It was sudden and it was immediate. It was reckless and it was dirty. The person went in fully clothed, with watches, with glasses, with wallets, in good clothes, in pajamas, in sweatshirts and jeans. Anyone who has ever gone into the water in fleece and denim knows- it is not easy to get out of the water, nor is it a pleasant feeling.

The evening always began like any other roast night; fun was had by all. Those of us that had been there for a long time, recognized when the subtle undercurrent that preceded the "throw-in", began to swell.

After the roasting and eating had finished, the adults gathered around the fire. The children disbanded throughout the woods with flashlights in hands and smiles on faces.

Wooden Adirondack chairs in many colors mixed with other chairs encircled the huge campfire. The fire was hot, the stars were brilliant, the smell of wood smoke and citronella was everywhere, and the echo of laughter bounced from the mountains. Happiness filled the mountain air.

The upright piano was uncovered from its protective canvas sheath. It was manned by our resident entertainer. Requests flooded in as did those campers who wanted to stand near him and sing piano-side.

Beverages flowed, voices rose in song, and the dancing began.

All of this entertainment served as a distraction for the unsuspecting soul. It was known that no man, woman or child was spared when it came to the waterskier's (or birthday celebrant's) rite of passage.

The group of campers who were the conspirators planned before the roast as to who was to be thrown into the lake. Sometimes it was only one, maybe two or perhaps three, but there were also times that it became one big, wet, free-for-all!

The men (it was always started by the men…) nonchalantly scattered and ambled toward the evening's 'subject'. They laughed, they cajoled and they chatted as they crept nearer their prey. While the chosen one sang, or danced, or drank *Snatch!* Next stop: the water.

This rite spared no one, regardless of gender or age.

It was not over as quickly as one would imagine. The chosen person seldom went willingly. There was no mercy shown when thrown in. He'd wiggle, he'd wrangle, he'd yell, and he'd bargain. All to no avail.

Sometimes the actual "throwing-in" was rapid and painless. Sometimes it was slow and torturous. Held by their feet and wrists, the recipient of the evening's fun and games was carried out into the lake until they reached a foot in depth. If the celebrant was a fighter, they were "flung" in. If a good sport, they generally got the "dip". Little by little, their body was slowly and uncomfortably lowered into the water

Once dropped in, the evening's person of distinction stood up flinging and splashing water at those that did the deed. The laughter, the hoots and even the applause, spoke volumes for the camaraderie and happiness that everyone felt. Staggering out of the water, with wet clothes, jewelry, glasses and yes, even pajamas…no one ever became truly angry or upset.

Some nights there were more than one on the schedule. And sometimes everyone ended up in the water. It was all in fun and it was a highlight every single week!

Oh, and the one in pajamas? They went to his cabin and grabbed him out of his bed!

Chocolate Ice Cream and French Fries
training tools for my LDL

Once upon a time, when my arteries were free and clear of the residue and genetic toxins that seemed to find its way into them, I loved ice cream and french fries. Chocolate, was the flavor on the ice cream wish list, and I found vinegar, salt and ketchup were the best culinary companions to shoestring potatoes.

***

Over the years, two places were built on site that served food. They were great little places, The Restaurant and The Beachcomber. Both did not exist at the same time, but both were great for a good time. Each of them was unique.

The Restaurant was first. I was in my pre-teens at the time it was in its early life. Meals were available, but we went for the ice cream.

It was absolutely delicious and it hit the spot on hot summer afternoons. My friend's older sister worked there and we went nearly every day. My friend liked vanilla in a cone, but I always had mine in a dish. It was in a small, icy cold, metal dish; the frost and condensation would form on it as I ate the chocolate confection. Just the sight of it made me feel cool- temperature, not attitude.

Mary Amelia Paladin

The building was wooden; it blended very well, almost camouflaged, into the group of trees in which it nestled. It was rather dark inside; a neon signature light was the brightest thing to illuminate one of the interior walls. Low wattage, pin up lamps hung above each booth. It was typical sixties, North Country restaurant décor, almost what is seen these days and labeled as "retro-rustic". The booths were quite comfortable initially, but the longer we sat on them, the more our skin stuck to them. When it was time to slide out of the booth, it felt like we had left the backs of our thighs behind. We tried to go there in mid-afternoon; we had already been swimming, so our suits and towels were wet. We put our beach towels on the oversized seats to save our legs the agony of feeling as though our flesh had been stripped from our legs. Not unlike the feeling we felt as we peeled dried Elmer's Glue from our fingertips each time we made something on a rainy day.

Music played continually in the background with The Dave Clark Five and The Four Seasons deemed favorites. As an only child, I did not know what teens were listening to and what was popular. Without an older sibling blasting the tunes on a record player, I had *no* idea; I was only eleven. My friend had two older sisters; she was "with it", and could sing along with the music just like the older girls who worked there.

By the end of summer, I was in love with Frankie Valli and the Four Seasons; I felt pretty darn cool once I learned the words to "Rag Doll".

***

The Adirondacks that are the Other Half of Me

The Beachcomber looked like part of a set in one of those 1960s surfside cult movies. It had all the telltale signs of sand, sun and surf.

It was fashioned like a walk-up snack bar with no interior seating. A small patio of blacktop served as its floor. In front of the counter, stools were secured into the hard surface. Draped from a roof that covered the counter and stools were yards and yards of fishing nets. The nets and ropes draped from beam to beam and were quite nautical in effect. They were not the type of nets that I had seen used in the lake; they were large, sheet-like nets. I assume typical of catching schools of fish perhaps, in larger waters than Brant Lake. Sea shells hung on the net, as did large cork buoys and other artifacts typical of being on the waterfront.

My favorite thing was the french fries. There was nothing like hot, fresh, french fries on a sultry, sticky, July or August afternoon…served with a Coca Cola on ice to solidify that fryer grease. Yum.

It was always busy. Most of those that sat counter side and huddled around the counter were young people. The music was upbeat, the kids laughed and teased each other; it was a great atmosphere. Just the kind of place Annette, Frankie, Gidget and Moondoggie would have loved!.

To the Big Screen
like swallows to Capistrano

Movies, shown on the beach, began in the sixties. How great that was. For those of us who spent the entire summers at the lake it was like a gift from above!

We didn't have televisions at the time, and even radio reception was poor. To watch a moving image on a screen of any type was *fan*-tastic! They were movies that had been released in theatres earlier, but we enjoyed them thoroughly. They were always family friendly: Disney, Alfred Hitchcock, John Wayne, and Elvis…all the top box office sellers of the era.

The screen was a huge, plywood-type square that was painted white. On movie night it was hung on an even bigger frame, which was made especially for it. Its footers were sunk deep into the sand. Behind the screen was the vast blackness, which draped the lake and the mountains on the other side. It was as dark as any theatre. The only light came from a small flame in the fire nearby and the hazy ray of motion that beamed from the projector's lens.

The title of the movie to be shown was posted in the store the week before. Everyone would talk about it. Had they seen it before? Was it good? Was it scary? We all waited for it as if it were a brand new, "never before seen!" movie.

On movie night, all the cottages and camps emptied out as everyone toted their chairs and refreshments down to the beach. It was a migration of happy, chattering campers. We also carried our blankets, just in case it got chilly, or the mosquitoes were hungry. Occassionally I sat with my parents, but mostly I sat with my friends; always, it was alot more fun.

One movie I remember vividly was "Wait Until Dark" with Audrey Hepburn. I had seen it in the theatre and I liked it very much. It was scary, but not brutal. I knew there was a part that was startling but I was prepared, I *thought*.

On that particular night, my friends and I sat on the overhang of a nearby cabin, The Shangri La, to watch the movie. It was a rather flat roof, about ten feet from the ground. There were quite a few of us up there and we were having a blast. Eating, whispering, giggling, and doing all the obnoxious, annoying stuff that teens do. But we did watch the movie too. All of a sudden, the jolt of the scary part caught me off guard (when the bad person jumps out at a blind Audrey). I screamed and jerked upward, which caused my blanket to shift underneath me and…down I went. All the way to the ground. Regretfully, I did not go down quietly. There was a thud, a groan, then *many* parents who gathered around me to confirm my safety. The movie (which had been stopped of course) resumed and everything went on as scheduled.

I, however, would have felt a lot better about it all had I broken a bone or, at least, been rendered unconscious.

Movie night

Objects are Closer Than They Appear
...so are mothers

When I was sixteen, like many sixteen year olds of the time, I was a smoker. Not a big smoker, a social smoker. I only smoked when I was with my friends, and I always knew that if per chance my mother caught me, things could get bad, in a hurry.

I had been invited to a sleepover at my friend's cabin one warm summer night. She was a bit older than I, but not by much. I had another friend of mine staying with us for the week so naturally, she was invited as well. She was younger than I was by two years.

The parents of the host cabin were not going to be home, but that was not a worry. In our small group of vacation cottages, everyone had known everyone else for years. It was a given that no danger would ensue. It was also more than a given, that if there were any troublesome activities undertaken by us, there would definitely be danger. That... of the parental sort.

The five or six of us at this particular sleepover were enjoying ourselves immensely. Talking, laughing, and of course, smoking. We did so quietly, because it was after midnight. We made sure the music was not disturbing. We did not laugh or giggle too loudly, and all was going quite well.

I sat at the end of the couch. To my immediate left was a window next to the entry stairs. My fourteen-year-old houseguest was on my right. The curtains were closed in secrecy but we had the windows open so we would not suffocate to death from all the smoking that was going on.

My houseguest friend had just lit a cigarette and held her pack out for me. I gladly accepted. I usually obtained my cigarettes from a half empty pack of my mother's Kent 100s. Never did I take any from a nearly full or nearly empty pack. The empty space was too noticeable. I had already smoked the three, to which I had helped myself, earlier that day. I usually did not have any "cigs on me" for long. We continued with our laughter, enjoying the feeling of faux maturity and freedom.

I had just placed the cigarette between my lips and struck a match to light it when a knock sounded at the door. Being that it was growing late, we got a bit frightened.

Instinctively I turned to my left to look and see who it could be at that time of night.

I parted the curtains. There, less than six inches from my cigarette toting face, stood my mother.

My eyes widened, my finger burned on the match, the unlit cigarette fell from my lips and I knew the end of my life was near. Her eyes did the same as mine and, without waiting for an invitation, came into the camp. I was, shall we say- gathered up, and told we were going home. Just she and I; my houseguest friend stayed at the sleepover.

We headed toward our cottage at what was a semi-rapid pace. My progression was not from my own power; my mother enthusiastically gave me some help. Upon arrival home, I was reminded that I was to have been a good example to our "young houseguest". I sat, I listened, I heard it all. Then I went to bed.

When I got in bed, I could not help but chuckle (just a little). I hadn't given it away. I hadn't even tried to talk my way out of it. In addition, I must say that I did enjoy the satisfaction of the thought of my friend, our houseguest, smoking her brains out in that cloud filled camp. I envied her just a little bit, but I was glad she was having the fun I could not.

I was caught. I was punished. I kept quiet. And yet I still felt as though I was the victor. My mom was mad at me…but I knew that would pass. It always did. As I drifted off that night, I am sure a smile creased my face. It replaced the pucker one gets from a cigarette, which would have been there had the end to my evening been different.

But…that was okay with me; I knew my friends would "have one for me".

I must add, I had a terrific mom. I pulled some "loo-loos" (as she called them) in my teen-aged years. How she did not disown me is a miracle at which I still wonder…

Panic in the Pits
sand, not arm

Breathless, he crested the top ridge of the shifting hill.

"Hey man, there's a cat out there with a gun!" His voice was a shaky, whisper-like yell. His eyes were wide and they darted back towards the deserted house we had passed an hour earlier. "He's sitting in the dark on the porch of that house. He has a rifle; we have to get out of here!"

My mind reeled.

Oh no…My parents are going to kill me! If "the cat" out there doesn't do it first, that is.

The sweat broke out around my neck, my chest, my back and my face. I was soaking wet in seconds and I had never been one to sweat.

It was in mid July of 1968; fifteen of us sat in the dark atop the mountain of sandy soil. When our friend said that, I swear I heard the massive air intake, as fifteen pairs of lungs gasped.

We were at the sand pits on Beaver Pond Road. We were not supposed to be there. No one was. There were "No Trespassing" signs everywhere, but that had never stopped us before. We went there to hang out- no parents, no rules, just laughter and friendship. Never would we have thought of this. We knew we would be punished if discovered there, but not *killed dead*.

The boys jumped up first and ran to the side of the informant; he was always the most dramatic person of our group, no doubt about it. We considered that when he said anything, but this time seemed different; he was visibly shaken and sweating profusely.

He had gone out of the pits and across the road to relieve himself a few minutes earlier. Apparently, on his way back over he caught side of "the cat with a gun".

One of the boys asked him to describe exactly what he had seen.

Who cares? I wanted to scream. *It doesn't matter what he saw-exactly!*

I just wanted to get away before "the cat with a gun" shot us.

The boys made a plan…we would split up into three groups and leave in three different directions. One group would crawl through the brush and woods behind the pits. The next had to cross the road and go through the woods to the back of the cemetery. The last group (because one of the girls had a broken foot and would have to be carried) had to brave it, and walk right out Beaver Pond Road-directly in front of the deserted house with the porch on which, "the cat with a gun" sat.

Great. There were five boys, which meant one of the groups only got one boy in their group.

Back then, and at that age, we all wanted boys in our group. We felt safer: I don't know why; that night they were just as scared as we were. Especially the informant.

The boys decided they would determine who was in which group.

What? Are you kidding me?

Naturally the informant was in the group going the farthest away from the road and…"the cat with a gun".

I, of course, was selected to go in the group with only the one boy. He would have to piggyback the girl with the broken foot.

So we have no boy that could save our lives, because the one we have will be busy…

Our lucky little group had to walk past the deserted house.

Oh boy, I'm dead…Either here or at home. It was destined to be. This is it, my last night on earth. July 1968, barely thirteen and I am staring death in the face.

The informant and his group were out of the pits as if a swarm of killer bees were on their tails. The second group crossed the road and rustled into the woods; we heard a splash as someone fell into the creek, followed by a chorus of stifled "shushes". We pulled ourselves together and took our time getting ready to go.

What's the hurry anyway? We have to walk right past "the cat with a gun" down the middle of Beaver Pond Road, straight to our untimely deaths. Who needs to hurry for that?

We helped the injured girl down the side of the large mountain of sand and onto the boy's back. She was a tall girl and the boy was not. Her feet nearly dragged on the ground, so we had to keep telling her to lift up the one in the cast. Each time we did, she giggled.

What the heck is so funny?

So, we started to walk.

We walked slowly.

No one spoke.

Someone giggled sporadically.

Mary Amelia Paladin

Oh, come on! I wanted to muzzle her.

The deserted house wasn't more than the length of a football field from the sand pits, but we were there so quickly it felt as though it had been only a couple of feet.

I began to feel sick to my stomach. I could not imagine that this could really be as bad as the informant said.

It's Brant Lake! Things like this don't happen here! The thought had run through my mind numerous times already that night.

When we were almost directly in front of the house, I suggested to one of the other girls that we shine our flashlights at the porch where "the cat with a gun" supposedly sat. There were three of us, plus the girl and boy piggyback team. I knew they wouldn't be able to hold their flashlights toward the porch but the rest of us could.

She looked at me and without one bit of hesitation and said, "Yeah, maybe we can blind him so he can't see to shoot."

Well, that wasn't exactly the reason I had mentioned it but...okay.

The three of us hung back; we let Giggles and her ride go on ahead of us.

By that point, I was not nauseous, I was not scared, and I was not going to back down.

We pointed our flashlights toward the porch of the deserted house.

Snap! Snap! Snap!

Our lights beamed right onto the porch. We waited a second for our eyes to adjust, and then the three of us squinted.

What is that?

Whatever it was, it did not move. It was big, but not solid like a person's body. We walked closer. And closer. And closer, until we were on the lawn right below the steps up to the porch.

We climbed the steps together. We breathed easily. We were not afraid anymore.

"Oh, jeeze!" one friend said.

"We should have known…" the other said.

Yeah…we should have…

There, on the porch, was an old, overstuffed chair. On the chair was a large, metal, rooftop television antennae perched on its side. The pole end was stuck up and over the side of the porch rail.

That…was the "cat with a gun" our friend had seen.

We looked at each other and laughed.

Typical.

Later that night we gathered back on the beach. When everyone found out what it was and that there was never any danger, the tale became legendary. We told the story all summer long as well as the many summers that followed.

If, by chance, you were to ask any of the fifteen people who had been there, I'm sure most of them have never forgotten, "the cat with a gun"!

The Cemetery
the theatre for fear

A short distance from Palisades Road there is an old cemetery. It has been there as long as I can remember. I visited it to pay respects to a few special people who are buried there and to visit the place where one would soon be laid to rest.

Then, I walked around a bit to look at the names of those I recognized who rest there for all eternity. Dahl, Denker, Hofmann, Mead, Meade, Persons, Ross…I know of other names that will find their place on carved granite in that small cemetery someday, but hopefully those will be a long time in coming.

A large tree, next to the fence, partially shades the tiny cemetery. There are bushes growing tall around another part of it. And on one side its opens toward a huge green pasture. Brant Lake is visible from that spot. The serenity of the place evokes the essence, and recognition, of lives past. Some are known to me, some not, but all vibrant in their existence.

When I was a kid, however, I am sorry to say I did not think about that. I guess most kids don't.

***

When we were teenagers, we would cut out from our camps frequently to go to the cemetery. I wish I could say it was done in order to contemplate the meaning of life, or the afterlife, or lives of those who passed before us. But it was nothing as benevolent as that…it was to scare the living daylights out of the new kids, the scaredy cat kids, and each other.

Saturdays were "changeover days", when the rental cottages changed occupants. Sometimes there would be only a few changeovers whereas other times all, or most, would get new families in them. Our cemetery outings mostly happened on Sunday and Monday nights. It was hard to get to know the changeover kids well enough by Saturday night so that they would go to the cemetery with us, but by Sunday…we had them.

Bravely we walked down Palisades Road, toward Beaver Pond Road. We told story after story. While still on Palisades, we kept it rather benign, stories of animal attacks and scary people who had chased us. However, by the time we turned on to Beaver Pond Road, (where there were no street lights) things were forbidden and evil. We made up stories filled with lies, or at the very best, marginal truths.

One starred the hermit from Pharaoh Lake. We told the new kids that he came out in search of food and would tear the sweatshirt off your back if you had one, so he could keep it for wintertime. We told them of the séances that occurred for generations inside the gates of the graveyard, stirring the souls of all that laid there; those who could not rest traveled between the cemetery and the sand pits all night, every night, looking for a way home. "One-eyed Jack" would sit in the dark and wait for unsuspecting kids to go past his house and shoot at them (a story that evolved from the "cat with a gun" episode).

The Adirondacks that are the Other Half of Me

We had a very good story of a ghost who stood in wait on one of the tombstones; he was not visible until he jumped on top of whomever was first to pass by it. We staged it by sending one of the boys in our group to the cemetery ahead of us where he waited on the branch of a big tree above a tall headstone. Dressed in black, he brushed frightfully close to the intended victim, wailed, and ran through the graveyard, out through the gate, and down the road.

When a few of us reached driving age, we left before the entourage began the journey and we went to the sand pits. We waited there until we heard their voices at the cemetery, a number of yards away. We tied sheets to the top of the car (to the roof, antenna, or hatch, whatever was the tallest part) and then drove down Beaver Pond Road, past the cemetery without headlights. We drove just fast enough to keep the "ghosts" afloat in the air. It wasn't difficult to see to drive, unless there was not a moon that night…then it got a bit hairy to be scary (sorry).

There was never any malicious intent toward the others. We thought of it as merely an extension of campfire ghost stories, somewhat like a field trip, in order to learn local lore. Everyone always had a great story to share. Once we were all back in front of the fire, it was amazing how "unafraid" everyone had become.

***

Just a few years ago, we (a friend of many years and I), decided that it would be great to give our kids and their friends the experience of a "real trip to the cemetery". We had both experienced the thrill, the fear, and the laughter of the adventure many times over in our youth. We wanted to make it something they would never forget.

We planned the whole excursion minute by minute; we decided we would need a lead person, someone to go ahead of us in the daylight and prepare the scene. Fortunately, my husband was there that weekend and was game to be that lead man. There are advantages to having married someone who grew up there because he 'gets it' and does not find it silly, or odd.

We spoke first, of course, to the parents of all the children and cleared the adventure through them. My friend and I led the unsuspecting, trusting, flock of kids (our own included) down Palisades in late dusk All the old stories resurfaced: the hermit, the animals, One-Eyed Jack, the whole script. My partner in scare tactics and I could barely keep ourselves from laughing. In fact, we had to separate in order to feign caution and fear; we could not look at each other, nor hear the other's voice or we would laugh. We reached the cemetery in the dark and we all entered, eighteen kids ranging in ages from nine to sixteen, and us.

It was not long before the kids were "hearing something".

"Over there, what is that?"

Thud…

"Oh No! What fell?!!??!"

"Where?!"

"I saw something move! There! See it!??!!?"

By that point, they hung all over all over each other, and us.

They were scared and we were suffocating. We needed to laugh; we could not.

"There...I see it! It is on the ground! It's moving!"

"I'm gonna hit it with this!" a large stick appeared in the hand of one of the teenaged girls and she stepped forward, rapidly.

"No! Wait!" from me.

I knew my husband, dressed head to toe in black sweats and on his belly in the grass, was in for a beating.

"Stop! You can't. The others ghosts will come out to save him! They'll come after you!" I lied.

She dropped the stick and I saw the bushes on the other side of the cemetery move, then rustle.

"Ohhh! The bushes!" A younger boy said, right before he lunged onto his older brother and both fell to the ground.

"I want to go *now*..." one of the other boys said. He did not cry, but he was close to it.

We rounded everyone up, which was not difficult, they were all connected to each other in some way. Hands, arms, sweatshirts, jeans. Everyone hung onto something belonging to the person next to him, or her.

We started back toward Palisades; the kids seemed more scared as we walked out Beaver Pond Road than when we had walked in. They looked for the animals, hermits, and one-eyed shooters.

We told them not to worry; we would protect them.

They told us we were no consolation. We could not run if we had to.

Wanna bet?!?!?

Once we reached the main road things got better; a streetlight and an infrequent car threw some light on our supernatural stroll. The kids felt better; they laughed and swapped stories of graveyard courage and knowledge of the impossibility of ghosts…

As we reached the little road that led to our camps, another set of headlights approached, then it signaled to turn in our road. We moved to the side of the road to allow the vehicle enough room. As it pulled in, I saw it was my husband.

What the heck?!?!?

He stopped next to us and started to chat. He responded appropriately to our daughter's inquisition as to why he was out in his car. Standing behind the group of kids my eyeballs were bulging and my head shaking back and forth in disbelief at his timing. We waved, he drove in, and we arrived at camp a few minutes later.

The kids' voices were loud and excited as they shared their experience with anyone who would listen. They reported the whole episode to my husband, the accessory during the fact. He ooh-ed and aah-ed in all the right places.

The level of enthusiasm was still high when everyone got ready to go home. Good nights were said as we all stood together one last time for the night, unified by our experience.

It was then that my husband opened his car door. It was then that, out onto the ground (in front of all the kids…), fell his black sweats, and hoodie.

Under the Shangri-La
di-da

Almost everyone has heard the song "Under the Boardwalk" recorded in 1964 by The Drifters. I was in 4th grade at the time so it made no significant impression upon me then, but later, it took on a completely new meaning.

To this day, every time I hear that song play on an oldies station (did I say "oldies" out loud?) my mind reels backward. Set in a different place and time the song could have been noted as a Brant Lake chart topper.

The Boardwalk song was written about a seaside hideaway where life all around it is practical and commonplace. In the secrecy of the hideaway, however, young love blooms. Our 'boardwalk hideaway' was under the Shangri-La.

Before I go any farther, to those of you who know exactly what I mean, have no fear- there will not be any cats let out of any bags.

An elevated cottage in design, the Shangri-La perched above the beach overlooking the water. Underneath its enclosed porch was an overhang or roof, that extended outward from the cottage. One end was enclosed, except for a window with no glass; the front and opposite ends, were open. The supports were semi-sculpted columns, which I presume were porch posts in a prior life.

I remember that there was an original use for the overhang, perhaps boat storage, but that was a bit before

I was old enough to note. During my years of awareness it served many practical uses.

In unexpected thunderstorms everyone darted boisterously from their spots on the sand, clamoring to fit under the roof of the Shangri-La. Giggles and false exclamations of disappointment rang out as the level of noise rose with the happy voices of campers, talking and laughing together. Crowded yet joyous, the vacationing comrades found every happenstance a gleeful experience.

On movie and roast nights, the red Coca Cola vending machine that was housed there was put back into service; although its automatic dispensing days were over, its refrigeration worked perfectly. Boasting its importance with its heavy door opened wide, cheerful campers picked their favorite flavor from it. With a snap and a clank, the cap popped off and fell into the metal tray on the door of the old red friend. That snap and clank became a sound that rang synonymous to me with events held on the beach.

However, the best times were on dreary, wet, afternoons. It served as shelter for the kids who did not want to miss one moment together by staying inside their camps. Cards were played, stories were told, friendships and romances developed. It afforded summer friends a place that was secluded, and yet not *too* secluded. Yes, there was also hand holding and first kisses, as well as heartaches and happiness. There was laughter there were tears. There were also friendships made that have lasted a lifetime.

"Under the Boardwalk"…a mega hit? Perhaps.

Nevertheless, for those of us growing up back then, the biggest hit, and one of the fondest memories was "Under the Shangri-La".

Christmas on the Beach
the offspring of three Bs…no, not bears

It started because of a birthday, a beverage and a brainstorm. It was developed by a small group of the seasonal mothers who were best pals all summer long, one of which was mine. From humble beginnings, it grew to be the big event of the summer for over fifteen years.

One hot, summer afternoon in 1971, a small celebration with cold **b**everages, was held on the beach for one of the summer residents; it was her **b**irthday.

Laughing, talking and having a wonderful time, as my mom and her friends always did, beverages or not, they decided it was only fair that those who had their birthdays in the 'off-season' celebrate at the lake too. One of the women had a **b**rainstorm; her birthday fell in December, around the holidays. Perhaps a Christmas party would be fun!

And so it began. They had a mission. A mission they took seriously. And those women were serious about having fun. They knew there had to be food. They knew there had to be beverages. They knew there had to be entertainment. They knew there had to be gifts.

The "committee", as they became known, went all out for the event. A Christmas tree went up, tables were gathered, and gifts were wrapped. Food was planned, husbands were directed, and costumes were made. Music was arranged-live and canned. Offspring helped too- willingly or not.

The food was brought by all the families in attendance to share with each other. The beverages flowed from every direction and in every form imaginable.

The entertainment came in all forms: piano, harmonica, banjo, singing, guitar, skits, and *always* of course...Santa! One of the "committee husbands" donned Santa's suit in the August heat and played the part indisputably. A few of the other husbands were elves! *That* was entertainment; one of them was over six and half feet tall!

The gifts were acquisitions of the committee's favorite Saturday morning excursions-garages sales. Often those outings wore well into the day if a businessman's lunch and liquid refreshment were enjoyed at Tom Carroll's in Chestertown. As years passed, sale finds were joined by personalized handmade gifts as well.

The committee spent hours upon hours writing poems that accompanied each family's gift which was then presented to them by Santa Claus. They were sincere but funny. They were written especially for the recipient family and the poetry played on a characteristic or funny episode in that family's life. My family received many presentations concerning my dad and his (missing) sense of direction.

I remember the committee members' remarks on writing the poems: they always "had a blast, and it was almost as fun as the party itself". They laughed until their eyes ran dry.

Every summer's party had a theme; throughout the years there was Hawaiian, Hollywood, Bicentennial, Circus, Western, Roaring 20s, and Nursery Rhymes, to name just a few. It was typical for more than 200 people to attend. Most came in costume, but without a doubt, everyone came in sincere friendship, and everyone had a great time.

From the youngest to the oldest, there was something for everyone. Singing, dancing, food, drink, laughter and fun.

Undoubtedly, it was the union of our little lakeside community and the sincerity of the people that night each year that made us all one big family. Not only were we family for that festive occasion on that August night, but also for the 364 nights that followed.

Christmas party on the beach: Santa & Elf present gift

Mary Amelia Paladin

"The Committee" Roaring 20s year

A "Great" Camp to Us
good things do come in small packages

Our camp is not by any means similar to the great camps of the Adirondacks that tend to come to mind when mentioned.

There is no huge Great Room. No moose or bear head looms above. The exterior is not hand hewn logs from the High Peaks with a decorative, ornate design inlaid above our door. The interior does not have an open loft from which the entire panorama of the floor plan is breathtaking.

In fact, the ground on which our little abode rests is not even owned by us but is rented year by year. This ground is special ground. It is the ground on which my life was nurtured, enriched and set free. It is ground on which I will walk for quite a few more years (I hope), and even if that is not the case, this ground has filled my soul and will be taken wherever it is that I will spend eternity.

***

We are only the second family to live in our camp. It had been empty for quite a few years. The family who previously owned it had three boys; but they grew and the parents did not venture north from Albany anymore. It was neglected. It was overgrown with weeds, and a big wooden boat decayed in the front yard. Vines, ferns and daisies tumbled down the beautiful stone wall, which I swear, cried for freedom from the twisted fingers that choked it. The paint that had been a rich gray, the shade of granite, was pale, dried and peeling. Day after day, year after year, the camp sat empty. It became natural to all of us that it appeared overgrown and sad.

One day my mother, coordinator of camp acquisition, made a phone call to the owners. She asked if they would be willing to part with their little camp on Brant Lake. Happily they agreed; a few days later it was ours!

That was in August 1974; things have changed considerably. This camp has not been empty one summer since, with a few winter visits thrown in as well. It is a place that has sheltered joy and sadness; it is a place filled with old and new memories.

As I write this piece in the summer of 2008, I am grateful for, and hopeful of, the years that I can soak in the peaceful repose that this place provides for my soul.

Our Camp

The Dark Side of the Moon
was also a teapot

It was July 6, 1982, my twenty-seventh birthday. The day started as did most summer days at the lake. Sleep late, hit the beach for tanning, swimming and skiing. Later, dinner out with my folks at an Italian restaurant. I had eggplant parmesan, my dad had veal scaloppini and my mother had a hamburger.

"Very, very, rare please. Just run a match under it," she would say.

My mom did not like Italian food; she was adamant about it. And she would tell anyone that she only liked two things Italian: pizza...and my dad.

Lakeside, later that evening, two of my friends and I sat around the fire and waited for the total lunar eclipse that was expected that night. To prepare for the evening's event, we decided to run up to my camp to get something to drink. We stocked up on wine coolers and sodas and got ready to head back to the beach. My parents decided they wanted to see the eclipse as well, so we packed some Schaefer's and grape Nehis in the cooler too.

On the beach, my friends and I sat in the sand; my folks sat on the bench that was built between two trees. We talked, we laughed, we sang. It was great fun. My dad had retired two years earlier and it was nice to see him enjoy himself.

Mary Amelia Paladin

My friends and I began to get a bit silly while waiting for the eclipse; it seemed like an eternity. We decided that we would stage our own eclipse in the meantime. My parents were the moon; my friends and I linked our arms in a circle, and we became the earth. We totally eclipsed my parents from sight (and yes, we sang Pink Floyd). It may all sound quite childish, but it is a night I will never forget.

We grew tired of circling my parents in slow motion so we began to do other antics that had a bit more action involved. Somehow, "I'm a Little Teapot" morphed into the routine. We performed it alone, we performed ensemble, and I performed it in (much forgotten) French. We steamed up, we shouted, we tipped. We poured slowly, we poured quickly, and we even fell down when "Ring the Rosie" entered the repertoire. We laughed so hard our sides ached.

The (real) eclipse finally did happen; it was magnificent. The night sky was so dark that the lake was an endless, black veil. Upon its resurgence, the sliver of light that embellished the water's surface was awesome (I am not fond of the word but, it was).

That night will always warm my heart. My parents are gone now. Their laughter and their aging, yet smiling, eyes portrayed their delight at sharing the bliss of our youth. The memory of that look in their eyes comforts me still. One of those friends became my brother-in-law. Although we do not see each other much- distance and life, can often do that- I will always see his crazy antics in my mind's eye and remember the hilarity he added to the evening. My other friend died suddenly the following year. I can still hear her laughter, I can still see her face, and I can still say that she was one of the funniest, and most honest people, I have ever known.

It was perhaps an eclipse of the moon that night all those years ago. Nevertheless, as the years continue to pass, nothing can eclipse the echoes of our mirth. The laughter that bounced from the mountain across the lake and into the vast beyond, connects us through time- forever.

The Big Rock
handy mountain

I cannot begin to guess how many pairs of pants I ruined, or how many times my knees bled as I climbed the legendary "Big Rock". It beckoned to all of us as children, no matter what our age. Lots of pants and lots of band-aids were used by lots of kids. The Big Rock was the status symbol of childhood independence; it was daunting and yet, it was enticing. It called to us in a way only we, as children, heard.

When I was still very small, I would try repeatedly to grab onto the narrow, natural ridge on the side of the mountain-like rock, and pull myself up. The smallest elevation made me happy; I knew I would make it to the top on my very own, one day. In the meantime, my parents gave me a boost up and I sat on the very tip-top of the enormous single mound of stone. I placed my feet proudly, into that ridge, and it felt as if I were on the top of the highest mountain.

As the years passed, I became big enough to scurry up the side of that boulder as if it were nothing at all. It became second nature to get a bit of a run started and in three big steps, voila, I was at the top in no time at all and without a second thought.

One thing never changed; all the years that I played on that rock with my friends, I always thought of it as a big rock. More easily accessible, yes. But it was still a huge, solid, mountain to us.

Not so long ago, one of my childhood friends came to visit me. She had not been to Mead's Cottages in thirty years. We took a walk around the little lakeside community. She wanted to see all the places we played.

We took a walk down to the Big Rock. The property on which it sits is privately owned now, no longer accessible to everyone. As we walked along the perimeter of the fence and looked in at it, a voice came from a short distance away. The owner inside the fence invited us to come in and look at our friend more closely. We declined but thanked him; we told him of our walk down memory lane and this was one of our favorite spots as children.

Next to the Big Rock, where a giant maple once stood, a campfire pit exists, our old friend, its backdrop. It is charred on the one side from the campfires that now glaze the natural ridge that boosted so many small feet.

My friend commented on how small it appeared. I agreed. It was, in fact, only four and a half feet tall, not big at all in comparison to so many other large rocks, boulders and ledges found in the Adirondacks.

As we walked away, I could not help but think of that big, old rock and to think about the many years it had been there. The years that it gave numerous parents the opportunity to give their children a boost to make their dream come true. The years that it gave children the opportunity to climb and giggle, and jump with each other as they reached the top of their world. Lastly, the opportunity it gives the family which stays warm by its side as the yellow glow reflects from its rugged surface.

The Adirondacks that are the Other Half of Me

No, it was not as big as we remembered it. Not by any means. But its size is incomparable to its purpose. There will be many more years for that rock, more than we will be able to tally. Perhaps, in its next use, there will be little feet with skinned knees attached, scrambling once again up its enormous side.

Recall with Fondness, What Was
observe with delight, what is

My best friend came to visit me for a few days at Brant Lake in 2007; we had such a great time she stayed a week. It was her first visit back since 1969, when she had come to the Adirondacks on vacation with my family. We were fourteen back then, heading into the eighth grade. Truly, an entire lifetime ago.

We arranged to meet at Stewart's in Chestertown. I knew there was no way she would be able to find our camp after thirty eight years. We were non-driving teenagers back then; there was no need to pay attention to directions. Our world existed at the far end of the lake in a small community that had everything we needed.

As I walked the aisles of Grand Union picking up a few groceries, I kept thinking back to 1969. We had watched the moon landing on a tiny TV that my uncle had in his camp, complete with rabbit ear antennae and considerable static. We swam, hiked, danced, sang, and water-skied (her bikini top went north!). We had hung out at the fire. She met all my friends and she fit right in; that did not always happen in our tight knit group of friends. We ate Spaghetti-Os on an afternoon when the rain dripped freely through the ceiling, into pots and pans. We laughed so hard our sides hurt. Her mom and grandparents made a road trip from Pennsylvania to visit us; her "Pop-Pop" died shortly afterward. All those things were so long ago.

Mary Amelia Paladin

I pulled into Stewart's and there she was. Thirty eight years since my best friend had been at Brant Lake. Thirty eight years ago since she stood in this beautiful region. She was as excited to be there as I was to have her there. We stood on the sidewalk talking about her trip and our feelings of delight that she was there again. It was as though we were fourteen again; I was anxious to show her around and reintroduce her to Brant Lake. We giggled, and we were silly. To us, no time had passed.

A few moments later my daughter and two of her friends pulled in. We reminisced all over again, this time with the young women. My daughter and her friends understood our sheer joy at being there together again; they had been friends since they were little. They knew the feeling. They did not think we were silly, weird or, goofy moms. They understood completely. The Adirondacks have that effect on people.

When we got back to my camp, the memories started to gush from both of us. We fixed dinner, sat at the table for a long time and looked out onto the lake. We talked again, just the two of us- no kids, no husbands- just us. The cabin we had stayed in in 1969 is right down the road and in perfect view of our current camp, so we told and retold our adventures of the "Bay Pines".

As we cleaned up after dinner, the power went out. The entire northern end of Brant Lake had been plunged into darkness. Not so many years ago, the loss of power was a common occurrence (and still can be in winter, apparently); but since "real electricity" came to our end of the lake, we have had good luck in the summertime.

The Adirondacks that are the Other Half of Me

I worried a bit (it is what I do well) about no lights, no flushes, no water. All this, on a day when I had company. Then I remembered: she was not company. She was my best friend and…she was back at the lake!

We went on to have a wonderful night without lights (or flushes, or water). We sat on the porch with candles everywhere and a bottle of wine; we talked about our adventures at Brant Lake, thirty eight years earlier. How remarkably vivid those adventures still were.

***

Most everyone has a best friend. Whether that person is someone from a long time ago, or a new one, there is nothing like a true best friend. If you are lucky enough to have a best friend who has been around for a long time, despite the times that life takes you in different directions, then you are one lucky person. I consider myself such; she's been around a *long* time, (I mean that in a good way) and she is a good friend.

Our children are grown now. Two of her three are married, and mine is stretching her wings. We can see our responsibilities and obligations begin to loosen up a bit. We are able to spend more time together and, although quite a few years have passed, when we are together, we don't behave any better (I mean, older!) than we used to…

Mary Amelia Paladin

My best friend and I at Lake George

The Passing of the Matriarch

July 14, 2008: two and one-half weeks before her nine-tieth birthday, the woman without whom our piece of Adirondack heaven would never have existed, passed away.

Ruth Mead was one of a kind. She was a tiny woman in stature but she was stronger in soul than many men ten times her size. She loved life; she always said every day was a beautiful one. She loved her family; one could tell that by the way her eyes lit up when she spoke of them. She loved people; her sincerity was genuine and plentiful.

She was born and raised close to the shores of Brant Lake and I am sure there were times that were not easy for her. This was very rough country then. She was not the kind of person who would ever give notice of hardship, difficulty or tragedy; I know she was touched by all of those and yet she continued to see life as a gift.

While pondering the use of the word, three of the definitions I found for matriarch are: a female head of a family; a woman who is the founder or dominant member of a group or community; and a highly respected woman who is a mother. Ruth was all of those. Moreover, she was effectively all of those with a kindness that flowed from an endless fountain.

Initially, I thought the use of the term matriarch was too stiff, too dominant, and too cold. I felt those would not be appropriate; they would definitely not do. But then

I realized they <u>were</u> perfect. She *was* the matriarch. She worked very hard for many years to create and sustain this wonderful place which exists on her homeland. She was, in a sense, a mother to everything that many of us have enjoyed for many years.

When I heard of Ruth's passing I cried, a lot. I knew I would when the day came, but I cried more than I had expected to. She had a long and healthy life. She had friends and family that loved and respected her. Almost ninety is a good long life. I knew, of course, that one day she would be gone. But when that day came and I got the message, my heart fell. Perhaps it was because she was a part of my life for over fifty years. Perhaps it was because she told me she thought of me like one of her own. Perhaps it was because when my parents died she comforted me to ease the heartbreak of this parent-less only child. Whatever the reasons, I will always remember her with love.

I know there was a very special place in heaven waiting for Ruth Mead; I have always known there would be. She earned it without any doubt.

I also know that she now smiles down on us with the quiet gentleness that was hers alone.

There Comes a Time
to go

Call me foolish, call me whatever you will, but I hope that I will always be able to call our camp "our second home". Certainly, age plays a role. Mobility, health, feelings, and who knows what...can all change in a heartbeat.

In the last few years I have watched sadly as some of my friends have decided to leave.

Times have changed. People have changed. It happens. Sometimes for the good, sometimes for the not-so-good; but for whatever reason, there comes a time when the realization strikes that it is time to go.

As I write this, it is as though I am speaking of anyone else (no, everyone else) but me. I may find that this will not always be the case, but I will dig in my heels, with the intent of preventing it.

Recently, I watched a friend of many years walk past our camp on what I think was his last walk from the beach. He and his wife had just sold their camp; times had changed for them. Their children are grown with families of their own. The distance and soaring fuel prices were a deterrent, and they were not using their camp as much as they had been in the past years. It had become economically foolish. When I had spoken with him and his wife, they rationalized their decision. It was a sensible one.

As I looked at his face, a face I have seen every summer at one point or another for over thirty years, a face in which I saw his father's face, long since passed, sadness swept over me.

It hit me that it will not be a given that I see him again next year, even though his sisters and mother still have places here. It cannot be guaranteed that we will talk about things we knew of years ago. And I will miss him.

Watching him round the bend and out of sight, as he made that last walk back to his camp, my throat tightened. I found it impossible to fight back the tears that trickled down my cheek. They were not loud, wracking tears; they were the kind of tears that break through futile resistance, to note the solemnity of time's passage. Times that were youthful, spontaneous and free.

And although my friend may not be able to come back to visit regularly, or at all, his spirit will always remain, as do those that have left before him. His presence here has left an impression on the spatial milieu, which will be one, with the cast of many, who have walked here. He has joined the legions of special people that have made my life, and this place, what it is.

Strength is portrayed in many ways and regardless of one's strength and from where it is obtained, it is still difficult to turn and walk away when the realization hits. And there comes a time...to go.

To Love a Place
music maestro, please…

How lucky I have been to have had the opportunity to become familiar with the splendor and the magnificence, that is abundant throughout this amazing region. Whether it is from the highest peak or fire tower, from the depths of the deepest gorge or lake, this is truly (as the saying goes) God's country.

I hope you have enjoyed these stories from the North Country. Maybe some day I will write about more of the adventures that took place here. I have had *the* most wonderful time(s) of my life in the Adirondacks. I wish the same for you.

If you are new to the region, have not explored much, or if you have never been to the Adirondack Mountains of New York state…it's time for a road trip to see what grandeur awaits you!

About the Author:

Mary was born in Danville, Pennsylvania. She is a lifelong summer resident on Brant Lake in the Adirondack Mountains of New York. An only child of a Scottish immigrant mother (who was thrilled to be a naturalized American citizen!) and a first generation American/Italian father, she celebrated in a family proud of its heritage.

She was raised in a home filled with love, pets, and the arts, which enabled her to develop a wide array of interests and abilities. Along with those experiences were lessons teaching respect for herself, for others, and for life in general.

Mary has studied various forms of art throughout her life: creative writing, poetry, pottery, sculpture, textile design, fiber arts and jewelry making. Painting, writing and drawing are her favorite forms of expression, with painting being her *passion*. She works in acrylic, watercolor and gouache.

As a young adult, she freelanced in the fashion and cosmetic industry, affirming the basis of her upbringing: that *true* beauty comes from within.

In her thirties, Mary became a wife and mother. She started a business, incorporating her paintings on giftware and commissioned pieces. It gave her the flexibility to care for her small child and aging parents.

Mary Amelia Paladin

Nearly twenty years later, Mary's business was destroyed by fire. She decided it was time to change directions, and return to her love of the written word. She uses her love of art as well in illustrations, designing, and teaching classes.

Her child is grown and her parents have passed from this world. She is grateful for each moment she has to experience what life can hold. Whether those moments are joyful or sad, they have been a gift that she will continue to gather and share with others.

Mary writes or paints everyday, whether she is at her winter home in central Pennsylvania, or her summer "camp" in the Adirondack Mts. of New York.

She shares her life with her husband, her daughter, and their pets- all of whom have been subjects of, or instrumental in, her favorite forms of expression...

The Adirondacks that are the Other Half of Me

1960: Brant Lake, NY

Loved it then- love it now!

CPSIA information can be obtained
at www.ICGtesting.com
Printed in the USA
BVHW030206300821
615576BV00014B/109